If everyone helps to hold up th[
then one person does not becom[

AFRICAN PROVERB

Holding Up The Sky

Love, Power and Learning
in the Development of a Community

TRISH BARTLEY

community links

By the time this book is published, many children, young people, women and men from Mashabela and villages like it all over Southern Africa, will have died. We are witnessing a storm of HIV/AIDS sweeping over the people of Africa, changing communities, regions, and countries forever – and leaving millions behind who are grieving and vulnerable. I pray that the hearts of those living in the North will wake up to the realities of people in the South and act in ways that acknowledge our responsibility, interconnection, and interdependence with them.

With the wish that the people of Mashabela are honoured for their courage, beauty, learning, dignity, presence, and love – I dedicate this book to them.

Community Links works to ensure that all contractors and agents producing our publications use papers of a natural recyclable material made from the wood pulp of trees grown in sustainable forests. The processes of manufacturing conform to all current environmental regulations.

A British Library CIP record is available for this publication

HOLDING UP THE SKY ISBN 09544047 0 X

All photographs by Trish Bartley, cover photograph of the Leoleo mountains, Limpopo, South Africa – taken near Apel

Cover Design by Simon Bottrell, 7Creative, 25 Ditchling Rise, Brighton, East Sussex BN1 4QL
Printed by Sheaf Graphics, 191 Upper Allen Street, Sheffield, S3 7GW

Contents

Preface

I f you are a development worker, this book is intended for you – wherever you work and whoever you work with. But do you consider yourself to be working in development?

'Development' is a term which usually refers to work with the poorest of the poor in the 'developing world'. People and communities in the North are considered already 'developed' – however ridiculous this sounds. But the processes, methods, and approaches used to involve people who are disadvantaged, excluded and marginalised, wherever they are, are very similar.

This book reflects on principles and learning in grass roots development practice. It focuses on an in-depth study of an intervention with ordinary people in an African village. As a practitioner, coming from a Northern community, I went there to learn. I wanted to discover whether the essence of the development process and practice was the same, whatever the culture, environment, diversity of people, and their needs.

Some of you, who work with local people in an urban or Northern context, may question the relevance of reading about a development intervention in a rural Southern village context. What can it offer you? I found when I compared my practice in South Africa with the way I had worked with local people in the UK, there was much more that was common than was different – once I had adjusted to the obvious vast differences in physical, cultural, and social context and needs.

I invite you to make the leap and translate this book with openness and curiosity so that it may be useful to you, in your own practice. People and their learning contain rich diversity and difference, but they also reveal important common threads. This has to be so – in the intrinsic humanity that we all share. It is time that we recognised that development practice from the South has much to offer those of us working in the North.

Here is opportunity to find meaning in development within a relatively simple process. Mashabela village was quite undeveloped and 'un-worked'. There are few opportunities now to look at development in the raw, so to speak, and to see the basics of participatory practice. In most places, history, conflict, and inter-agency or inter-factional struggle considerably complicate the picture.

Relationships and the connections forged within the development process are central to both the story and the learning of this book. Developing a person-centred learning approach that emphasised process, values, participation and self-development was at the heart of this intervention.

Of course, not all development workers see themselves to be in the business of developing people – or if they do, it is a poor second to the main business of development. But if process is understood to be as important as product, then involving ordinary people becomes an important opportunity to develop leadership, realise local capacity and invest in an area. I would argue that we ignore this at our cost.

By calling ourselves development practitioners, in the South and North, we are connecting a vast body of practice and can learn from each other. Currently, we only consider limited examples of practice from within our own continents or countries as relevant to our own work. This book challenges this assumption and invites reflection across a broader base.

Why Write a Book?

After 13 years as a community development worker in Manchester, I decided to go out to South Africa to research my own practice and reflect on what I had been doing for so many years. In a small way, I had developed some innovative approaches to working in the community that had had some measure of success. In exploring whether this was particular to the community where I had been employed, I sought to work in a quite different context to determine whether there was wider relevance. What follows is the story of that journey.

As a community worker from the North, I saw my role as one of facilitator. When the community group invited the local press to record the presentation of a minibus, my job was to stand behind the bus, out of the way, as the photo was being taken – even though I may have written the press release and co-ordinated the funding application. My role was to find ways of supporting local people to have more influence in their lives and to raise their positive visibility as leaders and role models in their community. They did not need me to become invisible within the process, but as the development facilitator, it would have been wholly inappropriate to lead from the front.

Writing this book and becoming visible within the development process has been very challenging. It has run counter to my usual way of working. 'Not me but them' I thought was my focus. But within the act of reflection, I have come to understand more about my own intention and development as practitioner. I hope this reflexivity will be of value to others. It is far from self-congratulatory – indeed the act of writing has often served to identify my doubts and deepen my questions.

I chose to write a book because of the impact of the experience on me, the learning outcomes that it seemed to contain, and the respect I held for the village people who let me work with them for nearly a year.

The Journey Home

It has taken a long time to complete the circle. I left the village of Mashabela at the end of 1997 and travelled home via Asia, visiting India, Sri Lanka and Nepal.

In Sri Lanka I met the highly respected Dr A.T. Ariyaratne, who founded the Sarvodaya Shramadana Movement in 1958, at one time one of the world's best-known development movements. Sarvodaya's aim has been to create a society that follows the middle ground between poverty and affluence. Drawing on Buddhist and Gandhian teachings, it emphasises the development of the whole person and an integrated focus on the social, psychological, and religious as well as the economic. 'Unless social change is brought about by people who are changed and uplifted in their hearts, they will be merely exchanging one set of problems for another, exchanging injustice for injustice, terror for terror, and hatred for hatred'[1] said Jehan Perera, a Sarvodayan worker.

When I met Dr Ariyaratne in January 1998, he had just returned from a conference in the Schumacher College in Devon, UK. I told him about my experience in South Africa and my focus on a whole person perspective in development. During our conversation, he encouraged me to remember the centrality of the development of the practitioner herself. As a Buddhist, he talked in terms of awakening and personal practice. Eighteen months later, when I was introduced to mindfulness-based work, I heard similar words. 'Teach out of your own practice'.

Whilst in Nepal, I spent ten weeks in a Tibetan Buddhist monastery, reflecting on my experience and meditating with other Westerners and with Tibetan monks and nuns. It was a rich time of learning and making meaning. When I eventually returned to the UK in April 1998, I was quite changed from the person who had left eighteen months before. The transition back to life in busy, crowded UK was difficult after the space of rural South Africa and the mountain monastery, perched up high above the bustle of Kathmandu. But within a few months, I found a peaceful cottage in North Wales to move into, at the foot of a mountain and in sight of the sea – a perfect place to write.

Six months later, as I was preparing to return to Mashabela to evaluate the development, I was diagnosed with cancer. Nearly twelve months of treatment followed and my focus changed to my health and my body, and learning what I needed to do to stay well.

I returned to the village in March 2000, still recovering from the effects of the treatment. For 10 weeks I interviewed those who had been closest to the centre of the development, now nearly three years earlier. Months of transcribing followed, but from late 2001, I got down to writing – interspersed with necessary gaps to develop a training business and earn my living. It took two more years to complete the book.

Being Present – Awareness in Development

The experience of these years has inevitably influenced my writing. There are many references to being 'present' and 'aware'. At a profound level, this is a demanding path of training that leads to realising the true nature of reality. However this takes many years or even lives – and is not the subject of this book!

The point here is to highlight the importance of cultivating awareness in every day life, especially in relation to work with others. This may appear nonsensical. How can we not be present in what we do? However, most of us, much of the time, are so busy 'in our heads', thinking and feeling, distracted by what has just happened or what might come up – that we do not give our full attention to the situation we are in. We have all had occasions when we have talked to someone, who seems 'miles away'. Even though they appear to be listening to what we are saying and are physically present, they are not really aware.

Being grounded in the experience of our physical senses and aware of the activity of the mind seems to be a key to being aware, open, and sensitive to people and situations around us. There are many barriers to staying with this awareness, but by working with them, we are more able to be with ourselves, the situations and people *as they are*, rather than as we want them to be – or believe them to be. This is crucial to some of the themes I have written about in this book.

Acknowledgments

I want to acknowledge my grateful thanks to the very many people who have helped and supported me with writing and producing this book – especially:

- The Woodward Trust and Camilla Sainsbury for their generous funding and support.

- David Robinson and Community Links for their ongoing support.

- Loretta van Schalkwyk and David Robinson for their stimulating and valuable essays.

- Richard McKeever for his publishing role.

- David Dalton of Commonsense Communications for his editing.

- Sheaf Graphics for their layout, printing and patience.

- Simon Bottrell of 7Creative for his cover design.

- Evan Herbert of Pistyll for his artistry and the baobab tree.

- My sisters Josephine Seccombe and Diana Allanson, who in their different ways offered me special and invaluable support.

- Sarah Madrid for greatly improving the village section and for her precious friendship in Sekhukhuneland.

- Peter and Elizabeth Anderson for wonderful conversations and weekly baths in Sekhukhuneland.

- Sister Lydia Pardeller and Father Patrick Gallagher for their very generous help and support in South Africa.

- Mashabela friends, especially Annah Mashabela, Altah Maroka, Elizabeth Metwane, Terdla Mohuba, Molefe Sello, Segapi and Nong Makola, Napé Diketani, Libra Chumu, M.J. Makanatleng, Marumo Makau and D.J. Makau.

- Sisters Kathleen, Christine, Eileesh and Elizabeth for their kindness to me at Apel mission.

- Those who have inspired and influenced me – especially Rigdzin Shikpo, Francis Batten, Ken and Elizabeth Mellor, Ferris Urbanowski, Linda Gwillim and Md. Anisur Rahman.

- Those who acted as readers and proof-readers for generously giving their time and valuable feedback.

- My friends for their special encouragement – especially Janne Foster, Paul Dunne, Sue Wells and Kathryn Schofield.

- My children Julia Bartley and Christopher Neil, who inspired and encouraged me.

- Roger van Zwanenburg of Pluto Press for his support.

- And to many others who in different ways offered an idea, an encouragement, or a conversation just at the right time.

And especially to Warren Banks, who with great patience held my hand and helped me find my confidence, courage and capacity to write much of this.

Mande Regina Mashabela

The Chief of the Mashabela Tribal Authority

Dear Reader

The coming of Manyaku has brought about many changes in my village. Her going up and down with the members of Mashabela Development Council has been seen as an empowering process. The fact that Manyaku is writing a book about the work we did with her in our village, will remain a guiding tool for the future. We hope that the book will be useful to everybody who reads it. We hope that they will learn much from our village.

Mande R. Mashabela,

Mashabela Kgosi (Chief) – May 2000

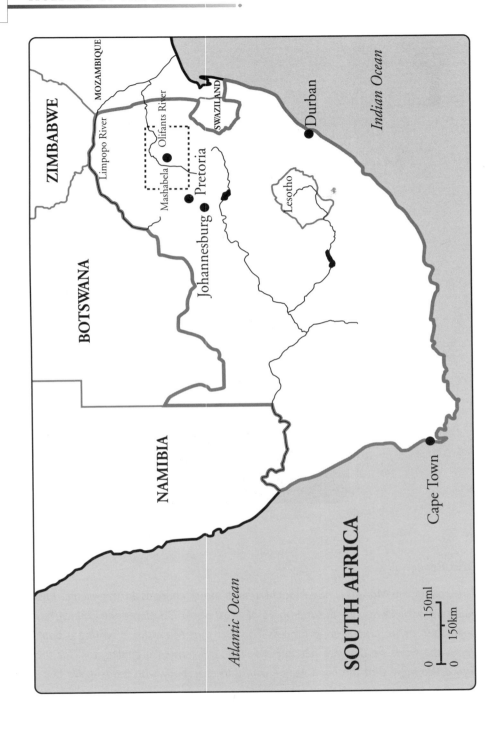

Introduction

> *When gold is in the mountains*
> *and we've ravaged the depths*
> *till we've given up digging,*
> *it will be brought forth into day*
> *by the river that mines*
> *the silences of stone.*

Rainer Maria Rilke[1]

As development workers, our job is to help other people to develop. However, we may find that *we* are the ones who learn most from the process. This is not wrong – even though it may appear paradoxical – for it is out of our own learning that we best enable the learning of others.

Our intention, in its fullest sense, underpins everything we do.

Yet when pressure and difficulties overwhelm us, it is hard to put into practice the things that we know sustain us and our practice. When needs are pressing, and problems and crises abound, we invariably move into reactive, automatic mode. From there, it is only a small step to losing a sense of balance and being unable to be fully present or skilful with people and their struggles.

But how can we justify spending time and energy investing in our own development as practitioners, when the needs of others are so great?

The development world is littered with idealistic, committed, and exhausted practitioners, who care little about themselves, besides their passion to make a difference for others. Self-sacrifice and grinding toil have become habitual. It is easy to understand how patience and sympathetic understanding gets worn away.

We have all experienced this.

The quality of our learning and the depth of our personal awareness lie at the heart of our integrity with others. This does not imply that the goal should be to develop a perfect practice or find an ultimate development truth. There is no such thing. Indeed, even trying to get it right can be problematic.

Sometimes just by staying open to people in their uncertainty, we are most closely connected to what is true – for within precious moments of mutual learning and interconnection, there is immense possibility for change.

Development Defined

Development supports people to be all that they are – enabling them to:

- establish and sustain their well-being
- experience their right to dignity and freedom
- express their capacity for creativity
- access power over decisions and resources that affect their lives

All too often, development is seen as an economic activity – a necessary response to poverty and exclusion. It is also viewed as a method for realising individual or collective potential – as a means of helping people overcome their problems. These development forms aim to raise people up, or improve them in some way – in relation to their health, education, livelihood, or some other area.

There is another way of seeing the function of development, which I have followed within this book. It is to consider people as already intrinsically whole, but who through circumstance or experience have become oppressed, excluded, and marginalised. This profoundly and adversely affects their ability to live dignified, free, healthy, and creative lives. The function of development then needs to include processes that support ordinary people to express who they are and put them at the centre of decisions and decision making that affect their lives.

'The tragedy of underdevelopment is not that ordinary people have remained poor – but that they have been inhibited from their authentic development as humans.'[2]

Purpose

The focus of this book is to explore the practice of development through the learning, awareness, and connection of the development practitioner and the local people involved in the development.

Writing in the spirit of congruence, my primary intention is to enable the learning of village people from the South to inform and enrich the development practice of people in the North (and the South). There is certainly much that I learnt from those who still have customs and ways of living that in the main, sustain connection and social networks – things that we, who live in affluent societies, have mostly lost. The picture is obviously a lot more complex than that, but it seems vital to me that we affirm our human interconnection in this age of globalisation, and respect and learn from those who have profound qualities we lack.

This started out as community development fieldwork research for a postgraduate degree. I chose to write a book, instead of a dissertation, in the belief that this would be more useful to me and my learning, and probably others and theirs. It is, in large part, a description of my own learning journey, written as a development story, intending to demonstrate that development practice is as much about the practitioner and her learning and the quality of relationships that she makes, as it is about the local people involved in development, whose communities are being 'developed'. In this way, my purpose is to invite reflection and ask questions about the practice of development; about the relationships formed between development workers and those they work with; and about the personal and professional learning of the practitioner herself.

I seek to emphasise the importance of the development worker's awareness of herself and her world as one of the key instruments of her practice. This is ambitious, seeking to encourage us to integrate our practice as development workers with the way we are in the world, both professionally and personally. Often, there can be a considerable gulf between who we are, and what we do and who we work with.

I also seek to celebrate and appreciate the skills, qualities, knowledge, and creativity of ordinary people. I believe that we easily diminish our own and others' abilities to be creative and courageous. So much in our world is dictated by material greed, dry intellect, or power seeking political discourse. In contrast, I want to share the words and actions of these economically very disadvantaged people, who speak with simple clarity. I want to demonstrate that development can be powerful, when local people are at the heart of the process and 'join hands' to work together for their mutual benefit. I hope to uncover the qualities and values that are needed for a genuine process of creativity and engagement that has the potential to offer benefit to a wide community.

'Community development, here in the North, has never been more important' as David Robinson of Community Links, writes in his fine essay at the end of this book. The gap between affluence and poverty – whether inside communities or countries, or globally across continents – is widening, still. This is outrageous alongside the scale of affluence in the world. Sadly, it seems, as people experience increased prosperity, most too easily become more self-serving and less compassionate towards others – whilst those who live in poverty inevitably become more marginalised and excluded. It is a profoundly dismal picture.

Robert Sampson, a Chicago sociologist[3], demonstrated a clear link between specific measures of 'neighbourliness' in communities and child health outcomes. The way people relate to each other affects both the basic measures of health and their own direct experience of well-being. We easily forget this in societies that value individual material acquisition much more than social cohesion and inter-connection.

Through this book, I wish to offer an example of community development that puts connection and relationship in front of the reader's attention, and show that even in the poorest communities, with basic resources and workable conditions, it is possible to work positively in ways that enhance learning and responsible local leadership. I want to enable those who are unfamiliar with development work to learn more about what it is and what it could be.

The community development practice in this book fits more into the context and framework of development practice as known in the developing world. The contexts that we work in, in the North and the South, vary enormously of course, but the practice I suggest, in essence, is similar. I hope that this book will make a contribution to linking our practice together, in ways that encourage us to learn from each other and from different contexts.

Finally, as well as laying out the tools of development, I also want to ask questions of practice and explore whether what is described here is or is not, a different sort of development. Through the exploration of some of the fundamental principles, I want to look at the way in which practice enables people to experience themselves, as whole human beings, in the wider perspective of a 'holistic' and integrated view of development.

Overall, this book is written in order to share the learning that came from this particular experience, and be relevant to development workers and others, from different contexts, who are interested in reflecting on their work and themselves. It might be a small and limited example of development, but the questions that are asked within it are relevant to wide application.

Content

Interspersed throughout the book are photo portraits of local people from Mashabela, and short statements, which they explicitly chose to articulate, to share aspects of development that they decided were most important for them. Their words are simple and genuine. They speak directly, sharing their feelings, ideas and learning about developing their village.

Chapter 1 introduces Mashabela and describes the physical, social and cultural context of this South African village, situated in the former Lebowa Bantustan or 'homeland' in the province of Limpopo (formerly the Northern Province and before that known as the Northern Transvaal). I introduce myself as development practitioner and explain my background in community development in the UK, my research goals, and my introduction to the village.

Chapter 2 tells the development story and outlines the events that took place in the village between March and October 1997. Included in this description are extracts from my personal journal of some of the key events. There are also outlines of some of the training interventions and processes that we used and a brief description of what took place after I left the village and what outcomes endured from our work.

Chapter 3 shares the learning that emerged from the development by reflecting on what happened, evaluating and reviewing the development stages, exploring the qualities of love, power, and learning that framed the research, and interpreting the learning in the light of models and theories that influenced the practice.

Chapter 4 draws together the principles and values that guide my practice, as a result of my experience in Mashabela, both before and since.

Chapter 5 is a short conclusion that revisits the intervention, with the aim of drawing the threads together in closure.

At the back of the book in Chapter 6 are two very significant essays, describing the context of development in South Africa and the UK. They are written by two development workers, with long and fine experience of their fields, who are well placed to describe the different character and challenge of development in the South and the North.

Loretta van Schalkwyk has been working with the South African development sector for many years, investing passionate commitment in the learning and development of people and organisations. Until recently, she worked for the leading edge Durban-based NGO, OLIVE, Organisation Development and Training.

David Robinson was one of the founders of the highly innovative and successful Community Links in East London, which has been working locally in Newham for over 25 years, and has been at the forefront of community development practice in the UK for over a decade. Their two essays highlight the current issues and debates within development and share the writers' vision, dreams, and challenges for the future.

Holding Up The Sky builds towards Chapters 3 and 4, the learning and the principles. You may read it in the order it is printed, or you can choose to move from chapter to chapter entirely as you feel inclined. Each chapter is complete in itself so the choice is yours. Start from the back if you like!

Background Issues

I have chosen to use the feminine form throughout the book whenever I refer to local people. In doing this, I am not intending to undermine the contribution of the village men to the intervention – but in wanting to use one gender throughout, it was an obvious choice to use the feminine 'she' and 'her'. This is a way of remembering the central but undervalued role of women in communities. It is also a reminder of the need to support and enable women to continue to open the doors of power, so that they can fully participate and share their special creativity and energy.

Soon after I started working in Mashabela, the village acting Chief gave me the African name of Manyaku. After this, most villagers took to calling me Manyaku – so I have used it throughout the book, as have local people in their sections when they refer to me.

I want to be clear that I do not seek to promote a specific practice model in this book. Indeed it is full of examples of practice and decisions that, in the light of hindsight and current learning, would probably not now be taken. However, it is, I believe, rich in reflection, and in examples of the natural creativity and courage of people who were open to learn from each other. It does not suggest that all ordinary people always behave in a way that is wise, trusting or good. But in the resonance of the intention to learn, there is always opportunity to transcend the ordinary.

Some of you reading these pages may question the values and practice of a white woman working in an African village. What sort of practice was this? Was she there to evangelise and convert local people, like the white missionaries she lived with?

You may feel uneasy about reading about the experience of a white person, working on her own with black people. It might be tempting to condemn her as a Northern imperialist researching development that is, after all, historically rooted in a liberal, colonial, capitalist world.

While these questions are important, I hope to show that it is possible to be white and work with black people, who are very different from yourself, in a way that does *not* reinforce oppression and prejudice – if sufficiently aware and sensitive. My intention has been to both write and work in ways that are as congruent as possible, and function from a position of respect towards those I work with. In doing so, my intention is to support processes of learning, empowerment and connection between us. It is for you to judge whether I succeed.

I invite you, the reader, to make your own translations from the context of this book into whatever is current and familiar to you, in your own experience. As I have said, this is not because I want to promote a practice model that can be transposed elsewhere, but because I believe the issues that came up for us in Mashabela are relevant to practice anywhere. It is easy to imagine that just because these people from South Africa were dealing with basic rural poverty issues of water, sanitation, women's participation, and so on – that they do not have relevance to urban settings or Northern contexts. The development content might be different, but the dilemmas, issues, learning, potential, and challenges share similar threads. Having worked at both ends of the world, I found this to be strikingly so.

When I was a community worker in Greater Manchester, before I went out to South Africa, I read very little about development practice in other parts of the world. There were few bridges that spanned the continents to link us. Happily there are more now. This book is one example, which is written in the spirit of honouring ordinary people everywhere. May the sharing of this learning that came out of Mashabela, benefit development practice and connect people wherever they come from.

'Most of us do not today believe that whatever the ups and downs of detail within our limited experience, the larger whole is primarily beautiful.'[4]

Delia Makola

My name is Delia Makola. I am 20 years old and training to be a teacher at Mokopane College of Education, near Potgietersrus. I am specialising in Maths, English and IT. I want to go on to do an honours degree, if I can.

I am the first born in my family and I have three younger sisters and one younger brother. My parents are called Nong and Segapi Makola. I was born in Mashabela and until I left for college, I have always lived here. I took my matric at Nkgonyeletse High School. I was one of the few in my year to get through.

When I was doing Standard 10, a lady, who was working for the sanitation project, came here and asked me to act in a drama to send a message to the people. We played it in three places. In the first place I was very afraid – the middle place was ok – but in the third place, I was very relaxed and playing freely. I knew that I was useful to my community. I felt great.

Now I am empowering the students who registered for part time study because they failed their matric. I called them together and talked about it and told them you have to do this and that – you have to read – and you are going to pass. That's what I told them. It is a beautiful small project for learning. What was in my mind was to advise them, to motivate them, because I know that they are no longer motivated. They think they are dull or something like that. So I called them and we sat together. I told them that they are good and intelligent.

At home by sitting down with me and telling me I am unique, I felt empowered by my father. I felt loved by him and considered special. If somebody's empowered, she does things wholeheartedly. She knows how important, how valuable things are. She feels recognised and valuable.

I am very proud of the work my father does in the village. He is an example to me. I am on the Boarding and Lodging Committee at the college. 'Why are you going to be on this committee?' he asked me. 'Father' I told him, 'I want to see what I have inherited from you. I want to prove myself'.

I think that empowerment helps people have visions. They start to think about other people.

Wherever I am, I usually compare it to my village. If I see something beautiful then I think ok, how can I do this in my village? If something is wrong, I say how are we doing this in my village? If it is the same way, I think how can we develop it?

We have a saying: 'Unity is the Power'. It is a vision that we will be fulfilled when we are together. We are going to make it. When the village is united there is no idea that gets lost. Every idea is useful. But if you propose an idea, you need to explain it so that everyone understands.

We are struggling to develop our villages. We need to be dedicated to the work we are doing. We need to be responsible and accountable.

In Africa we have Ubuntu, which means 'A human being is a human being because of other human beings'.

This makes sense to me. In everything that you do, you need inspiration from other people. Villages fail because people forget where their roots are. They are what they are because of the environment they grew up in.

I can say that my village is my treasure. It is the roots from which I grew. Yes. I am proud of it.

My message to people about development:

'Empowerment helps people have visions. They start to think about other people'.

ONE

Introducing the Community and the Development Practitioner

'Women hold up half the sky'

Chinese Proverb, widely quoted in South Africa
during the Fourth World Conference on Women held in Beijing, in 1995.

This chapter introduces the places and people whose lives, learning, and condition occupy the centre of this book. It sets the scene for the development story that follows. Themes and issues are described that affected the lives of Mashabela people as they were in 1997, when as practitioner I started working with them.

The Village of Mashabela

Sekhukhuneland – Off The Map

BACK IN 1996, when I first knew I would be spending a year in an area called Sekhukhuneland, I dug out the atlas and found the Olifants River, curving through an area north west of Johannesburg that looked quite empty. I visited the library of the School of Oriental and African Studies in London, and even contacted a specialist map shop, but without success. I could find no reference to Sekhukhuneland.

Before I left the UK, a friend found the area on a CD Rom and we printed off copies. I took them out with me to South Africa and showed them to local women, realising how significant it must be to see your village on a map for the first time. By then I had discovered that the area was far from empty. Indeed, it was densely populated with hundreds of villages.

You reach Mashabela on the R579, a tarred road that allows rapid passage through the former Lebowa 'homeland'. The R579 bisects the central part of Limpopo (formerly the Northern Province), from Polokwane through Lebowakgomo, in the north, to Jane Furse, Nebo and Glen Cowie in the south. Lebowakgomo, the former district capital, now caters for middle class Africans who work in Polokwane, the regional capital just to the north. Travelling south on the R579 out of Lebowakgomo, you pass an informal settlement – common to the outskirts of most towns in the former 'homeland' – tiny dwellings made of cardboard, paper, plastic sheeting, and scrap, packed closely together, without windows or water.

Thirty miles south of this settlement is Mashabela, and the transition from the majestic Leolo mountains, mountains north of Lebowakgomo, to the scrublands surrounding Mashabela is stark. Though not mountainous, the land around Mashabela is dotted with 'koppies', huge cairns of boulders, many quite high that resemble the building blocks of passing giants, but for the cactus and scrubby bushes clinging to life in the clefts of the rocks. But many years of deforestation have left the flat to rolling veldt bare, only occasionally interrupted by acacia trees, their long, white thorns visible through the dusty green leaves. Even rarer is the mature shade tree, and along the road they offer welcome respite from the elements to farmers and travellers alike.

The extreme deforestation has affected the climate as well, which is now semi-arid. Elderly residents of Sekhukhuneland describe the landscape in the early decades of the twentieth century as lush, with abundant streams and bush, fruit and foliage cover. The relative aridity of the region is long-standing however, and many of the same elders reminisce that in years of great hunger, their only resort for food was the once abundant prickly pear cactus, valued for its ability to withstand scouring drought. In addition, the near total deforestation of the area, in the context of dramatic climatic swings of drought and flooding, has contributed to widespread and devastating erosion of the topsoil. Driving along the R579, it is common to pass great rents in the earth, through fields, etching away hillsides and crumbling and washing away the fragile topsoil that still remains. The whims of El Nino and La Nina, minor irritations to many residents of the North, are devastating to the people of this region, bringing in turns crushing drought and the crop failures and hunger that follow, and torrential rains that pulverize local crops and flood great swathes of land. Hunger is the inevitable outcome for most residents in rural Sekhukhuneland.

It is easy to see why South Africa's annual road death toll is one of the highest in the world. Among drivers there is little regard for the posted speed limits, or for the faint lines indicating safe passing zones. Along the R579, mini-bus taxis ply their trade up and down to Polokwane, often dangerously laden with passengers and travelling at high speeds. Donkeys or goats amble freely across the road; on chilly nights, cattle often seek the slow-leaking warmth of the asphalt. Driving is hazardous for the unwary.

The R579 is fast and straight, and cuts Mashabela in half. It is a thoroughfare for pedestrians too: children walk down the road or cross it on their way to and from school. Women walk beside it with water containers or large bundles of firewood on their heads. They cross it to water their vegetables or tend their crops, often with babies on their backs. Youngsters too small for school but old enough to run an errand, use the road to reach the local spazas (storefronts built into the side of a house, or a small cart filled with basic goods). Accidents are inevitable, and fatalities are not uncommon.

Historical, Social and Economic Themes

In interpreting the former 'homeland's' past, one crucial context is the link between the workers, who migrate to the cities for jobs and their families in the villages. This connection, though changing and not as it once was, still influences the economic, social, and political development of villages like Mashabela. The core of the apartheid system was its ability to coerce labour from the remote 'homelands' to come to the gold and diamond fields and white urban centres for long periods of time. By denying the possibility of sustainable employment for blacks within the 'homelands' (by not allowing the development of a manufacturing or any other significant industrial base), the system ensured that people would have to leave the area, often travelling hundreds of kilometres, to find steady employment. Migrant labourers were rarely given more than an annual leave to return home to their villages. But their monthly remittances were a critical factor in the local 'homeland' economies and the livelihoods of individual families and networks of relatives.

With the challenges to the South African economy in the years following the 1994 elections and the attendant high unemployment rates (particularly in the former 'homelands'), this crucial support system has suffered significant damage. One consequence of this changing relationship is the high number of households who live in poverty. It is now more common for a household's income to derive from a granny's old age pension than from the remittances of a migrant husband or son. As a result, more and more households are headed by elderly women who are surrounded by a constellation of young relatives, usually the children of her sons, daughters, nieces, nephews, or cousins, all of whom are dependent on her meagre monthly income. Since many men and increasing numbers of women still move to the cities to follow the hope, however faint, of finding some form of employment, these grannies are often the sole remaining adult in households filled with dependent minors. The problem of AIDS orphans, discussed in greater detail below, only compounds these trends.

The other important theme is the crushed expectations of young people, who were brought up to believe that education and a new political order would offer them opportunities their parents never dreamed of. Following an example of activism set by the generations before them, many young people became politically active in the lead up to the 1994 elections. They worked hard raising political consciousness to mobilise strong ANC support in the villages.

As things have evolved, however, most young people now are worse off economically than their fathers were in the days of apartheid. Living in a rural area, with poor local schooling, further reduces their chances of finding work, and most young people leave for the cities, where jobs are scarce. Young women are now also involved in this exodus, although those who are single mothers stay behind in the village, unless they can find a family member to help with child care.

Not only do most young people find themselves with virtually no prospects for employment, the limited family income and non-existent personal income also prevent them from achieving the status traditionally required for true, social adulthood: marriage. As a result, the number of unofficial liaisons has swelled, followed logically by the number of children born to women without husbands.

The Chief and the Village Structure

There are few signposts on the road, but there is one to Ga Mashabela – Moshate – the home of Mashabela's Kgosi (Chief). Mashabela is referred to as one village – but in fact, it actually consists of nine separate sub villages and over 8,000 inhabitants, who are in principle loyal to the same Chief.

The degree of power and influence held by the kgosi in the rural areas has changed enormously since the 1950s, when 'chieftanship', although by no means without its critics, remained the central value in the society'.[1]

In 1972 the Lebowa 'homeland' was granted self-governing status by the apartheid government. The success of this manipulation depended on the co-operation of village kgosi, who were bought off. This was resented in the villages and led directly to the 1986 revolt in Sekhukhuneland, which was described as 'the most significant rural uprising for three decades'.[2]

There are five branches of the Mashabela Chief's family, which originate from the five wives of the last great Chief, Kgosi Nkgonyeletse, who ruled over Mashabela in the 1940s and 1950s. A full Chief can only come from the first family. After the former Chief died in 1997, Hunadi, a young woman was accepted as Mashabela's chief. It is still fairly unusual to have a woman as Chief and she is a candle wife – a princess from the neighbouring village of Mamone, who married Chief Nkgonyeletse after his death. This may appear odd to us from the North, but it is a not uncommon practice in the villages. The Catholic priest from the mission officiated at the marriage ceremony. Hunadi has now taken a partner to father her children and her eldest son will be the next full Chief of Mashabela.

The previous Chief (who died in 1997) was generally supportive of village development. He had given his blessing to an unusual village structure, ahead of its time. This was an amalgamation of the old civic Mashabela Tribal Authority, which was composed of village head men and elders – with the newer Mashabela Development Forum, which involved wide representation of every significant network in the village. The resulting Mashabela Development Council on paper was very impressive with a structure that involved and included everyone. However the executive was inevitably still dominated by men.

In 1997, Transitional Local Councils (TLCs) had just been appointed to act as a bridge between the Northern Provincial government and the villages. Regional NGOs worked out of Polokwane and another settlement called Jane Furse, but none, apart from the Rural Women's Association, who worked with the women in the gardens, the pre-schools, and the emergent women's resource centre, were actively involved in Mashabela. In former times, village development had focussed on the efforts of the migrant workers, who collected money from other villagers in the mines or factories to build village schools.

In the past, rent for land was paid to the Chief, who officially owned all the village and chose who could farm and build on what area. Now, the village Chief receives a salary from the state. Land distribution and reform is the responsibility of NGOs and government agencies. Land reform is a very live and contentious issue, inevitably fuelled by the difficult situation in neighbouring Zimbabwe.

Mashabela Infrastructure and Housing

Aside from the R579, there is only one other road in the village, a dirt track that leads from the R579 to the village of Mpanama. There are no bridges across the Olifants River. When the water levels rise, sub villages across the river are cut off, and their inhabitants must wait for the flow to subside before they can return to school, or reach the few spazas, churches, or transport centres on the other side of the river.

When I first started working in the village in 1997, there was no village water system of any sort. A very poor system, designed for the Chief, had long ago collapsed. Every household collected water from the river, or from local springs.

One woman told me that she fetched her water from different sources, depending on what it was to be used for. An outbreak of cholera some years back had led to concerns about safety – although very few families boiled their drinking water. This would involve more firewood collecting and add to the women's already impossibly heavy domestic burden.

In the remote sub villages, the water situation was even worse. In Maololo, there were two village wells, badly polluted by the animals. In Ga Selepe, water was drawn from a mountain stream, which often dried up in the winter.

In 1997 there was no electricity in the village and only the Catholic Mission and the hardware shop had generators. A few households had refrigerators, which run on gas cylinders and were used for special occasions. There was no public telephone. The Mission's phone was erratic, as the line was often brought down by people using telegraph poles for firewood.

Housing in the village varies greatly in style and size. The poorest dwellings are made from corrugated iron with no windows – stiflingly hot in the summer and very cold in the winter. Most others are built of home made bricks, using sand from the riverbed. Some houses are larger and better finished with painted plaster rendering. Most roofs are made from corrugated iron, the sheets held down with large rocks when nails are too expensive. Only the newest and most expensive houses along the R579 have red tile roofing, often owned by middle class families, who have a second house in the village to return to.

Some houses are built close to the tarred road, others are found near the dirt road or myriad walking tracks that wind their way around the villages. Single storey school buildings stand out in red brick, with overhanging roofs, which reduce the heat inside the classrooms. There are a few small shops, or 'spazas', in Mashabela that sell the most basic provisions such as bread, tea, soap, cigarettes, matches, and of course, the ubiquitous Coca Cola. The village hardware shop has a larger and wider selection and there are, inevitably, the bottle stores, which sell beer and other alcoholic drinks. Families with a regular income, such as the teachers, go to Polokwane, 100 kilometres away, to do their shopping at 'month end', when they have been paid.

All houses have yards, where the family gathers, under the shade tree if there is one. The yard is a typical feature of the mud-brick houses with either plastered floor or clean-swept dirt, and stuccoed benches built along one or more of the walls. Children play here in the sun, the elderly or infirm lie nearby, and residents in their courtyards hail passers-by for news or other greetings. Some households grow corn and vegetables, as long as the yard is large enough, and the garden area is protected from marauding goats. Some have fruit trees, and a fenced area where the goats are kept at night. At the lowest point of the yard stands the pit latrine, usually made of corrugated iron.

At dusk, a pall of smoke hangs over the village as families cook their meal, burning the firewood collected from the mountain under a pot of mealie meal (maize porridge). Better off families may be able to add chicken, beans or vegetables to the pot. Some cook with paraffin inside the house, and some buy coal to augment the firewood. Most rely on firewood, which is free.

Despite a long history of hunger, including several serious famines in the early and mid-twentieth century, and high levels of stunting and wasting amongst children recorded by the hospital in Jane Furse, few inhabitants acknowledge this history openly. There is said to be little serious malnutrition, now that protein supplements are given out at the local clinics and families are encouraged to add peanut butter to the mealie. Free school meals, a significant government initiative, have improved children's diets – but under-nourishment is still common, and hunger a part of daily life for most.

Education

By requiring that all teaching be done in Afrikaans (or English) (a decision that triggered the Soweto uprising in June of 1976), the apartheid system denied most black Africans, but particularly those in the rural areas, a decent education. Most of the current government were educated in a few missionary schools, where the training was more rigorous. Things have improved since then, but there is still a long way to go. Class sizes in most Mashabela secondary schools are high, and the school buildings, mostly old, are run down, vandalised, or damaged. In addition, most schools in Sekhukhuneland are grossly under-resourced and under-supplied, having too few desks, texts, blackboards, or even chalk.

A predictable consequence of these conditions is that exam results are low. In 1997, fewer than 4% of the students in standard 10 passed matric in the largest Mashabela secondary school. Without matric, the chances of getting a job are remote. Those who do pass have to fund themselves through university or college – a huge family undertaking – although loans are now available from the government after the second year. Free teacher training, traditionally the most popular option, has resulted in an oversupply of inadequately trained teachers.

Another legacy of the apartheid era education system is that most adults over 30 have never attended secondary school and over 50% of the older people in villages like Mashabela are illiterate. Free adult education courses are held in the Women's Resource Centre run by state funded adult education projects, but due to exhaustive household responsibilities, and low levels of confidence, take up is low. While education is a government priority, it will take a great deal of funding, training, and inspiration to raise the standard of rural schools.

Families and Rural Household Livelihood

When I first came to the village in 1997, family planning was still viewed with suspicion. Many women had five children or more, though younger couples seemed to have smaller families. Historically, women became pregnant when the men returned on their annual leave, usually at year-end. But as HIV/AIDS spread during the late 1980s and 1990s, a growing number of women became infected as the men brought the infection home with them from the cities. However, in 1997, HIV/AIDS and awareness-raising work around issues such as safer sex and contraception was in its very early days, and any discussion that included sex, among adults anyway, was not acceptable.

As of 2003, the impact of HIV/AIDS in the rural villages is vast and most families will be affected directly or indirectly. Despite this, there is still much shame connected to the disease. It is now the highest cause of death in young people and by the time the pandemic runs its course, AIDS will have changed the overall demography and life expectancy of the African population profoundly. Extended families are now raising large numbers of AIDS orphans and it is not unusual for grandmothers to be bringing up 10 or more grandchildren.

Along with the instability, caused by the HIV/AIDS health crisis, comes the marked instability of households' sources of income. Households draw on a variety of livelihood sources that often change from month to month. Employment in the village is almost non-existent. Poverty seems inescapable, unless you are a teacher, or have close ties to someone with a job in the city. In 1997, there were no viable village projects that contributed to family livelihoods – except the women's gardens, which produced important vegetables to eat and occasionally to sell. Most families have no regular wage – and those that do, may well be supporting very large households. Many families would simply not survive without the grandparent's monthly pension. I knew one family of seven that received R120 a month (approximately £12 then) from the paternal grandmother's pension. This bought them a monthly sack of staple mealie meal and some tea and sugar. It was their only regular income source and many months, it was all they had.

Beyond old age and meagre company retirement pensions, the 'homelands' have never had access to adequate social support networks provided by the government, and family networks have always had to fill in the considerable gaps. As the economy worsens, the relationship within the family is increasingly important in determining whether pleas for help are fulfilled, or even considered. Blood ties are generally more important than those of marriage.

Long-time neighbours without family connections are another common source of support for struggling families, and their help most frequently takes the form of food aid. The most vulnerable members of any community are those women who 'marry into' it, without the benefits of close blood ties or long term residency, and whose husbands have work in the cities and are not around to ensure their welfare.

While extended family networks are not as close as they used to be, there remains a practice of sharing food with a neighbour who is hungry, or giving money, if you have it, to a friend in need. Helping a family member may no longer be as common as it once was – but the extended family is still an important source of support and belonging.

Women and Gender Relations

'Women are disgraced by our culture' I was often told, although the men who would quote this, had little or no real understanding or awareness of the full disparity of status or responsibility between men and women. The daily domestic grind of the women bears this out. In comparison, many men who are out of work seem to do very little and have no clear role. The stereotype of the women working in the yard – washing, cooking, fetching firewood and water, feeding the children, tending the crops – while the man sleeps under the shade tree, is not a fallacy. Yet unemployed men bear a heavy burden as well, especially psychologically. Traditionally they are the providers, dominating the political and social webs of the village. Stuck in the village, unemployed, many without the status of marriage and unlikely to ever have the means to be able to marry – they are reduced to idleness and prey to destructive temptations.

In village meetings, men invariably dominate the discussions. Women attend but rarely contribute very much and tend to defer to the men. On their own, the women are more confident, at ease, and well able to participate and make decisions.

Churches and Religion

Many people in Mashabela consider themselves deeply religious, and church going is extremely important to them. There is an abundance of different village churches in Mashabela, separated by belief and practice, meeting place (often under a tree), and the colour of their uniform.

A Roman Catholic Mission was established in Mashabela in 1953, and the priest from the Mission was one of only a handful of whites allowed to live in the area in the days of apartheid. The 'Romans' (as the villagers call them) have a large and impressive church, which is attended by many of the better-off village people, such as the teachers. Irish missionary priests take their gospel to 25 far-flung 'outstations', supported by parishes at home in Ireland. Over the years, the Mission has developed a number of projects for the women, mostly initiated by the work of the Rural Women's Association in Apel (30 kilometres away), where there was a sister mission in 1997, run by five Franciscan missionary sisters.

Many other churches also exist. Some have their own communities, where buildings match uniforms. Some are based on 'born-again' principles with strong moral edicts, dietary restrictions, and anti-drinking rules. Some include ancestor worship and focus on shamanistic healing. Most households are linked with one church or another – although young people sometimes get drawn into their own evangelical sects.

Health and Healing

Up until 1999, a health clinic was run from a building in the Mission, staffed by two nursing sisters. Local hospitals at Jane Furse (15 kilometres away) and Glen Cowie (30 kilometres away) served the area. Once there, treatment was free – but getting there by taxi was expensive and only possible during the day. In 1997, both a new village clinic and a new hospital in Jane Furse was in the process of being built – both funded by an extensive government health programme.

Many local people still rely entirely on traditional healers when they are ill. Sangomas, sometimes disparagingly referred to as 'witch doctors', use 'muti' – medicines made of herbs and other ingredients, and throw the 'bones' to make their diagnoses. Sangomas are both feared and admired. Prophets are also traditional healers and as church members, often use Bibles and prayers alongside the 'bones' and 'muti'. In Mashabela, there are many traditional healers, who have their own network, which links into the development structure.

Village Development

The Rural Women's Association (RWA), based in Apel (30 kilometres away) was the only NGO which had developed projects and services for the women of the village. The women's gardens, which were started through a partnership of the women and the RWA, served an important function of both improving diet and bringing village women together. At the time that I first started working in Mashabela, the Women's Resource Centre was being developed by the RWA for the women from the gardens and others in the village. The centre later offered a range of projects and services such as cookery, sewing, adult education, and other training. It took a traditional approach to the training needs of the women, but was and still is an important development for those women living on that side of the village. Inevitably the close relationship with the church meant that most, but not all the women involved, also attended the mission church.

Later still, a project was developed for children with disabilities, and this was also held in the Women's Resource Centre and run by local women, and supported by the Catholic Mission. The premises of the centre were given to the women by the nearby Mashabela Primary School, who having an outstanding headteacher, was able to raise funds to improve school buildings and facilities, and raise the standard of the children's education. The support given by the Mission to the school has been an important factor in its success.

Years gone by, high profile village development focussed on the activities of the men who worked away. They pooled resources and collected money amongst themselves which was then used to buy materials to build schools in the sub villages. Most village schools were built in this way. The then apartheid government took over the salaries of the teachers once buildings were finished.

There were also a few examples of village initiated development projects. A brick building project started but sadly failed, when funds were misappropriated. Several agricultural projects were taking place in the sub villages, which were co-operative ventures amongst the villagers, who combined forces to help each other out and develop a patch of land together. One of the finest examples of village enterprise were the burial societies, which were run by the women, as thrift societies, to which families contributed in anticipation of the costly expense of family funerals.

Each church had fundraising schemes to build or buy uniforms or develop a new project. Despite the extensive poverty, there are endless small collections of money taking place all the time for a host of causes. Before I started work in the village, there were no NGOs working there, apart from the RWA – but in every corner of the village informal networks were busy planning, collecting money and taking action in small ways, to improve the lives of the villagers.

Leisure

Most leisure activities involve singing, and music is a very important part of village life. At the weekend, parties are held to celebrate births, weddings, initiations and funerals. Exuberant singing accompanies almost every occasion in the villages, and the unaccompanied four-part harmonies, sung in church, are a joy to hear. Hymns are also sung at the start and end of every village meeting.

Amongst young people, football is very popular, with sub-village teams regularly competing against each other. It is also becoming an important spectator sport in the village.

Most village leisure is also quite unstructured and includes passing time talking to friends at the spaza whilst on an errand, dawdling on the way to/from school, hanging out at the bottle store or at Moshate, engaging in various crafts (beading skirts for initiation, knitting, sewing, carving), going to church and praying, attending burial and other society meetings. In addition, co-operative work whilst not strictly leisure time is highly social and contributes to an important sense of connection and well-being. This might take place beside the river, where the washing is done, at the fields during periods of planting, weeding or harvesting; at church during initiation months; whilst collecting firewood; herding cattle; or cooking; or making African beer.

Summary

Mashabela is a colourful, friendly and lively place – full of activity and noise. The sense of inter-connection between people is a powerful characteristic of the village, despite inevitable conflicts, grinding poverty, and rapidly changing times.

Unique as this community is, its people face similar issues to those faced by communities all over the world. These include low and insecure incomes, poor infrastructure, and inadequate health and education services. Local people are unsurprisingly frustrated with the government at the slow pace of progress. There is a sense of helplessness in the face of global economic forces and the seeming inevitability of the HIV/AIDS epidemic. All this impacts on people in the village and leaves them with a sense of having little control over the forces that affect their lives.

Elizabeth Metwane

My name is Elizabeth Metwane and I am 43 years old. I am married with four children – all girls. They are 23, 13, nine, and five years old. My husband works away in Germiston. He returns home once a month. I sometimes work as a spiritual healer.

In 1997, I was a member of the Learning Group and one of the organisers of the Women's Conference.

I was the vice chairlady in the garden for nearly four years. Then they turned me into the chairperson for the Mashabela Woman's Resource Centre.

We started planning this garden in 1994, with Sister Mary. It was a difficult job and we were not sure at the end that we would be where we are now. We started by cutting and chopping the thorn trees and some big trees. Then we made a fence and after that we had to dig down for the pipes from the river to connect with this dam at the Mission. It was a very heavy job.

We started with 90 women, but some left, then we had about 60 — until we produced some veggies — and then they saw that the heavy job was finished, so some of the (original) women came back. We now have another garden, where we plant corn. The school gave us an old building in 1997, which we have renovated as a centre, where we train women for book keeping, chicken rearing, vegetable gardening, sewing, cooking, knitting. When we have knitting and sewing courses other women are welcome too.

Love plays a part in the village. If this was not the case, we would not involve the ladies who are not from the gardens. We would just hold the knowledge for ourselves. But we don't want to do that. We want to spread it to each and every woman, because we love our village.

Let the people of Mashabela work together. Do not hide or feel ashamed of yourself. Before we had the Learning Group we just took ourselves as useless. The Learning Group exposed us and took the women from the darkness. I have seen a difference in them. I myself have become more confident and am no longer shy. I am now one of the leaders.

Part of my learning is in my job in the garden and the centre. It benefits my children. They get veggies and I sell some too. My children learn from me and then they too become more confident.

I felt proud to be chosen as chairlady of the centre. I am also exposed, because a lot of people need my help. I put myself on the same level as them, so that they can feel free to come to me. There are a lot of ladies who don't know how to read and write and they feel 'small' at the meetings. I say to them 'You must feel free. We need your ideas. So when you are with us, forget about writing and reading and knowing other languages. The knowledge you have, is very useful to us'.

I help people to feel confident and brave. They believe me because I am free with them and my face is open and I am always smiling. I try to explain things to them first. I think they trust me because I say what I do. In my heart I am always happy if I can help someone. I think I am intended to help people.

The benefit (of helping people) is there for me, but it is hidden. As you see in our village, we are poor. We need money, but for so many years we have worked without having what we need. We have the promise of funding for water, but we still do not have electricity or telephones. We don't produce very much. I haven't got enough money. I want to be able to pay for schooling for my children and for their uniform and to be able to pay my societies. I want to do what others do – not to stay behind.

People fail when things come slowly. Some people have got short tempers, and say that things are not coming quickly enough. Then they withdraw. Others just want to help themselves and they stop trusting each other.

I would feel so happy if the village was united. The job would be simple. We could get the things we need, like water and electricity, much more easily.

My message to people about development is:

'The main thing is to work hard and trust each other – this gives you a lot more resources.'

The Development Practitioner

This section explains how as practitioner I found my way to Mashabela to work with local people in developing their village. It describes my background, my research goals for the South African work and how I found my base in Limpopo, formerly the Northern Province, with the Rural Women's Association. My learning reflections that came out of this experience are developed later in Chapter 3.

Finding My Way to South Africa – My Community Work Background

After graduating in sociology and philosophy at university, I went into social work as a Child Care Officer, as they were then called. Some years later, after having my children, I started work part time as a Voluntary Service Officer, recruiting and supporting volunteers with the Social Services Department in Stockport, part of the Greater Manchester conurbation, in the north-west of England.

Within a year of starting, I managed (with a co-conspirator) to engineer the role away from volunteers towards development work, which had much more potential to support real change. A couple of years later, I was in full time work, with the job title of Community Resource Worker, in Brinnington, a large estate on the outer edge of Stockport.

Through my time there, I learnt a lot about the rewards and challenges of community development. Brinnington was the 'poorest' ward in the borough and ranked tenth most disadvantaged in all Greater Manchester. My job was to bring groups of local people together, and support them to improve the quality of their lives and the lives of those like them. Projects were developed that harnessed local people's ideas and built their confidence, skills, and experience. Whatever the issue, local people were central to the process. My role was to support them to have more power in their lives and constantly try to find ways of including people who lived at the margins of the community.

Sometimes this resulted in initiatives such as the Credit Union, a form of community savings and loan bank, which involved every estate network and was entirely run by local people. This sort of development was very popular with local churches and town politicians. Other more sensitive areas like HIV/AIDS prevention – in which local people ran a needle exchange, supported families with AIDS and educated young people about safer sex – were harder to get supported.

Sometimes my role as a council employee came into conflict with my values and role as a community worker. During the first Gulf War in 1991, I was instructed not to develop a peace group in the local library, since it might be viewed as 'political'. This proved to be small fry compared to the dramas of supporting the needle exchange, which ran every Friday night next to a borough-wide special school for children with learning difficulties. The press had a field day when they found out, and some drugs workers, who felt threatened, waged a long campaign to discredit it. They failed, I am happy to say, and local people are still running it, all these years later.

I was fortunate in my managers, one especially. He was a qualified social work manager, interested in the potential of community development. He and I manoeuvred our way through many challenging situations and managed to keep more or less on track with the politicians. Without him, my job would have been very difficult. He encouraged me to reflect about the work I was doing and in 1990 I took an action learning Diploma in Management at Manchester Polytechnic, which was to prove a useful foundation for my South African research.

I was also lucky to have a rich and varied bunch of estate colleagues and over the years, developed a close supportive network. I was based with a team of child protection social workers, whose role was very different to my own. They often dealt with the results of family failure and trauma, whilst I tended to work with people's positive development capability. This led to challenging times between us, but after some years, we developed ways of working and discussing things together that was usually based on respect.

In my borough-wide community work team, there were wide variations in how we interpreted what we were trying to do. With some important but rare exceptions, I found myself out of tune with most of them, most of the time. Our practice values seemed to differ widely. In principle, we all wanted to work in ways that benefited excluded and disadvantaged people, but the way we translated this into practice varied a good deal.

I found that I was not primarily interested in changing things through organising ways of fighting the system, although inevitably this was sometimes necessary. I was more invested in supporting and harnessing the energy and enthusiasm of people. I found that by nurturing this momentum, people together could sometimes achieve extraordinary things that had the potential to transform their lives. It seemed to me that this dynamic for change was much more vital and creative than one where people cohered around blame and disadvantage.

My twelve years on the estate was a time of considerable personal change. Various life events triggered me into pursuing my own development and learning. I did this through a range of activities that included physical therapies, such as yoga and shiatsu; and emotional and psychotherapeutic person centred approaches. Through these I gained new understanding about both myself and others. I eventually took this further to follow a spiritual path of meditation practice that linked 'Western' psychotherapy with ancient eastern meditation practices. This was to prove very important – and offered me insight into ways of working with others that supported their development and well-being. I sought ways of bringing different therapies and approaches to the Brinnington estate with some success.

Over time, my close estate colleagues and I built up a tradition of community development work on the estate. Public health reports regularly mentioned the value of this in reducing morbidity and mortality in the area. This was encouraging – although it felt like an uphill struggle much of the time, with the impact of the 'Thatcher years' under the Conservative government 1979-1997 and the widening gap between affluence and disadvantage.

Twelve months before I left Brinnington, the Policy Planning Unit of Stockport Council suggested that we develop a regeneration partnership on the estate, with a view to attracting substantial funding from Europe. With local people at the centre, driving the partnership, it started well – but money, prestige, outside expertise and a rapidly deteriorating process overcame the early promise.

It was time to leave. Twelve months later in South Africa, I heard that the Council, having never filled the vacancy I left, had decided to disestablish the Brinnington community development post. When I heard the news, I reflected sadly on the way decisions are made by people in offices, who want to protect hard-pressed budgets. But a community development process is a bit like a garden, which needs plenty of time to get established, but left untended, is soon overtaken by weeds and reverts to how things were before it was first cultivated. I hoped this would not be the case in Brinnington and that local people had sufficient experience and leadership now, to tend the development of their community themselves.

Finding My Way to South Africa – Developing a Research Proposal

By 1995, I decided to take the plunge and leave my job to spend a year in South Africa researching development. My children were leaving home and it was a good time for me to venture out too.

I had worked in community developmen for over 12 years, but since my management diploma, I was mostly too busy 'doing' it, to reflect much about it.

I started to spend time in Manchester Central Library, reading development literature. Despite, or maybe because of, being in the field for so long, it was rare to come across something that offered me genuine insight, or that questioned or shifted my understanding.

One such article, by Md. Anisur Rahman written in 1990, influenced me more than any thing else at the time. In *The Case of the Third World: People's Self-Development*, Rahman argued that 'by focussing on economic needs... development discourse gets trapped in **negative thinking** and **dependence orientation**'. He outlined two views of development. The 'consumerist' view that links to liberal philosophy. This is formed by concepts of the economic needs of the person, which invariably depends on successful sections of the population (elites) delivering to the less fortunate. The 'creativist' view of development discourse, on the other hand, links to the socialist philosophy of Marx and others. This sees the development of the creative potential of a person as a basic human need, which expresses 'the primacy of human dignity'.[3]

This set me thinking – about poverty, equity, the relationship between developing the person and developing the community – and about the process of mobilising and engaging people in expressing their own ideas for change. Rahman, in his article, encouraged me to reflect on what it is to be fully human and how to bring these ideas into the heart of development practice. This is what I chose to underpin my research.

I registered at Lancaster University to do a part-time M.Phil and eventually sent out letters and information sheets to contacts in South Africa. I explained who I was and attempted to be clear about my research – through the questions I had formulated:

- What are the conditions that enable local people to be successful in tackling the issues that matter most to them?

- What helps local people to work together in ways that increase their opportunity for peace and well being?

- What factors increase people's involvement in decisions that affect their lives?

- How do community groups support the 'whole development' of their local people?

I asked projects to contact me if they were interested in using my experience in exchange for an opportunity for me to carry out my research. I tried to be clear about how I wanted to work. I was worried about the effect of breezing into an area as a researcher and then leaving again with lots of data and learning, but little or no benefit to local people. I began to realise how tight my time frame was. I planned to spend just under a year in South Africa.

The letters went out in March 1996. In early June, I got a phone message on a crackly line, inviting me to 'Just come, Trish. Come to us in South Africa'. She said that her name was Sister Mary and that I was welcome to stay in her Mission. She had accommodation for me, and lots of projects, she said.

First Visit to South Africa – Durban and the Northern Province

I took two weeks off in August to visit Sister Mary and the Rural Women's Association (RWA) in Apel, in the Northern Province of South Africa (now known as Limpopo).

I first went to Durban and stayed with Loretta van Schalkwyk, who worked for Olive, an organisation development and training NGO, who had passed on my initial information to Sister Mary and others in Limpopo.

My few days in Durban were fascinating. Loretta had arranged for me to meet a wide range of people and projects, so that I could get a feel for the development context in South Africa. I met Peter Derman, who was working in the University, helping communities negotiate with government departments over their infrastructure needs. He suggested that my research could act as a catalyst to help local people reflect on their stories and their own conditions. This soothed some of my concerns about the effect of my research on local people.

I learnt about funding difficulties in the development sector, and the drain of able black people away from NGOs into government. I saw evidence of the vast disparity in income and opportunity for different peoples. I heard anger and frustration at some of the government policies, after all the struggle, and fear that it might yet end in disaster. 'It's hard to hold the hope of the world' was a telling remark made to me. I became aware of the growing threat of violence in the cities and noticed the multiple burglar doors and locks on the houses. When Loretta lent me her car, she insisted that I drove with locked doors. All this was very new to me and offered insights that were both provoking and alarming.

I then flew via Johannesburg to Pietersburg (now known as Polokwane), in the Northern Province (now known as Limpopo), and spent six days in the Mission in Apel with Sister Mary and her Rural Women's Association, known as the RWA. Initially, I was pleasantly surprised by what I found. I had been concerned about the physical facilities and had wondered how I would cope. I found it was physically a whole lot better than I had expected, with WCs, bore hole water in the taps and even electricity, some of the time.

The village of Apel itself looked dry, dusty and desolate. I was very shocked by the poverty, which seemed quite as stark as in the plastic informal settlements that I had seen on the hills above Durban. I had little to prepare me. Everything was very different from what I was used to.

The contrast of the green around the Mission was startling compared to the rest of the village. Mary had planted the Mission with trees, beyond which was the women's vegetable gardens. Beyond them were houses and yards with precious little green vegetation, consisting of dusty plots with marauding goats, which ate everything in sight.

The RWA was very much Mary's enterprise and in some ways it appeared to have achieved exceptional progress. In only a few years, projects for women had been established in villages all over the area for many miles around. Most of these followed traditional lines of women's gardens, sewing projects, cookery and education courses and pre-school development – but traditional though they may be, they were much needed. However, the RWA tended to be run in ways that reinforced dependency and its methods even on cursory acquaintanceship were traditional and 'top down'.

There was much to consider but after some reflection on my options, after my return home, I decided to take up Sister Mary's offer of basing myself with the RWA.

On December 29th, I flew to South Africa and spent New Year in Cape Town with friends. I arrived in Apel on January 11th 1997 with a large backpack, laptop computer, printer and a student visa to stay for a year.

Life in Apel – Finding My Way to Mashabela

I was given a little wooden guest house set up on stilts on the edge of the Mission yard. Positioned opposite the convent, it was a palace compared to the two-room house I was expecting to live in.

It had four diminutive bedrooms, a tiny kitchen with a tap, sink and cooker, and a small veranda, at the front.

Outside, around the corner was a toilet and shower. The kitchen window at the back looked out across to the poultry project, more gardens, and the new clinic building site, beyond the Mission fence. Further away, you could just see the majestic Leolo Mountains far in the distance. Best of all, the house had windows on all four sides, which made the most of any available breeze. The roof was made of corrugated iron, which amplified every sound and when the rains came, the noise was deafening. I arrived in the height of the summer, when temperatures sometimes reached mid-40s.

Within a couple of weeks of my arrival, I bought a second hand car in Polokwane, which I was told would hold its value well when I came to sell it at the end of my stay. It was an invaluable resource, offering me precious independence, as local transport was unreliable and very risky.

Within a short time, I started work with Daisy, one of Sister Mary's key project workers, in the nearby village of NgKwana. She was developing a women's' resource centre, which would offer training, support and a range of activities for local women. We ran a village meeting together, and successfully recruited a group of women to develop the centre.

For nearly two months, things went reasonably well. We did some preliminary training and Daisy and I and the women seemed to be getting on quite well. I was learning about the culture and life of the village women. However, by the end of March, it was becoming clear that the project was not as independent as I had thought.

On April 1st, I found that the local women running the project were not going to be allowed to make their own decisions and that Mary had her own ideas about how things should run. I talked it over with her and we came to an understanding that I needed to find a project of my own. She agreed that it would be best for me to work independently from the RWA whilst continuing to live in the little wooden house within the Mission yard.

A week after I had first arrived in Apel, Mary had organised funding training, for people from all over the area who were active in the RWA or other development projects. The training was very ambitious and I found it difficult to understand. I wondered how local African people, for whom English was a second language, were managing.

Attending the workshop gave me a perfect opportunity to meet local people. At the first workshop and again when a second ran a month later, I met a man from the village of Mashabela called John Makola. I was later to know him by his African name of Nong. He invited me to come to his village to meet people active in development. He knew I was looking for a community development project, and he was keen that I should consider his village.

We set a date and I met with him and some of his colleagues in Mashabela Primary School. A few weeks later, on April 7th, I ran the first of several workshops for the Mashabela Development Council. Thirty-one village people attended, over half of them women.

M.J. Makamatleng

My name, Majatladi means 'conductor' in Sapedi. My middle name is Joseph. I am 40 years old and married, with three children. I have two boys, who are seven and four years old and a girl, who is nine.

I am Head Teacher at Nkgonyelste High School, which has over 1,000 pupils.

I was Chairperson on Mashabela Development Council in 1998 and for some time after. I have been active in village development since 1995.

In 1997, I attended a lot of workshops. I think I was really empowered. I am now able to address people and chair meetings. Sitting or standing I feel grounded. I have the power to talk to people – without hesitation. My heart beats well without any fright. I have confidence in myself.

It took time to adjust to attending workshops. Initially it felt so strange. I had to ask myself 'Am I going to cope in these development activities'? But as time went on, I realised that this is a very good thing to engage in. I thought that working with people was difficult. People have different ideas and different attitudes and different motives. Bringing them together is very tough. I thought I won't be able to do that. But as time went on, I realised that this is an easy job, as long as one has got commitment and is willing to take on challenges.

Before, I was somehow shy. I couldn't address many people. I couldn't mix with many people. But through those workshops, I had to adjust to be among people, to talk and to lead discussions. Previously I was somehow isolated. I think I have learnt a lot.

By empowering other people I'm trying to make development a continuous process. Even if people move away from this area to urban areas – they will continue with development. If I open my heart, I will learn and gain experience and be capacitated in development activities.

Development itself is a learning process. No-one can say I have now learnt enough or I am totally developed. I have learned as an individual — as MJ. It is helping me in the running of this school. I learnt a lot from the leadership workshop. I think I have gained as an individual and the community has gained from producing a person of my calibre.

Love is very important. Even though Mashabela is underdeveloped, I need love to develop this village. When we first talked about love in workshops I thought it was the love between a girl and a boy. What kind of love is this?! I listened with surprise – and then it came to me very simply, that this love was co-operation and accepting other people. It was not new — but in the context of development, love was new. The feelings were already there.

If you are a leader you have to be available – for the community to be able to use you as a resource. Whether they have some experience or not, you have to accept people. They are human beings like me. I have to help other people, because one day I will need help, for instance during bereavements. Money is not so important then.

This village is rather scattered through its sub villages. Those from Malagasane never considered those from Maololo as belonging to the same village. They saw

Maololo and Ga Selepe as isolated and apart. We were undermining the people who came from there.

Even though the village is disjointed, we are able to bring people together and they now realise that they belong to one community, that is Mashabela. We realise that we have to work together – because working as individual sub villages, it is very difficult to get services. We appreciate one another much more now.

I think it is important to involve people in identifying their own problems and coming up with possible solutions. No one can come from outside and develop this village. People have to do it themselves. I think that the knowledge that we have will help this village for many years in the future.

My message to people about development:

'People from the North have to take people from the Southern tip of Africa, for example us, in Mashabela village, as capable people in terms of development. We can teach them things about development. Even though our village is underdeveloped, they can learn from us.'

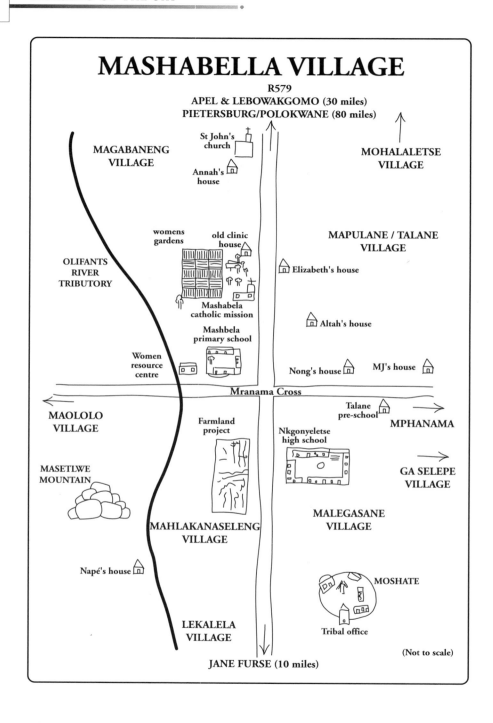

MASHABELLA VILLAGE

R579
APEL & LEBOWAKGOMO (30 miles)
PIETERSBURG/POLOKWANE (80 miles)

St John's church

MAGABANENG VILLAGE

Annah's house

MOHALALETSE VILLAGE

womens gardens

old clinic house

MAPULANE / TALANE VILLAGE

OLIFANTS RIVER TRIBUTORY

Elizabeth's house

Mashabela catholic mission

Mashbela primary school

Altah's house

Women resource centre

Nong's house   MJ's house

Mranama Cross

MAOLOLO VILLAGE

Farmland project

Talane pre-school

MPHANAMA

Nkgonyeletse high school

MASETLWE MOUNTAIN

GA SELEPE VILLAGE

MALEGASANE VILLAGE

MAHLAKANASELENG VILLAGE

Napé's house

MOSHATE

Tribal office

LEKALELA VILLAGE

(Not to scale)

JANE FURSE (10 miles)

TWO

The Development Story

*Look at every path closely and deliberately.
Try it as many times as you think necessary.
Then ask yourself and yourself alone one
question…Does this path have heart? If it
does, the path is good. If it doesn't, it is of no
use.*

Carlos Castaneda[1]

*This chapter recounts the development of Mashabela during 1997. The section
below outlines the key dates with the events. The following section describes the
development activity in the village, with stories from my journal interwoven into
the text. There are also tables, which describe the processes that we used.*

Key Dates and Events, 1997

January	11th	Trish arrives in Limpopo (the Northern Province)
	21st	Nong Makola meets Trish at Apel
March	1st	Mashabela Village Development Council established
April	7th	First Development Workshop. 31 attended.
	30th	Development Learning Group first Meeting.
May	17th	Mashabela Development Council Meeting – agrees to development proposals.
June	20th	Chief dies (2nd Workshop postponed).
July	1st	Second Development Workshop – 24 attended.
	5th	Chief's Funeral. 1,000+ attended.
July		Mashabela Village Meeting. 200+ attended.
	9th	Women's Conference Planning Group starts weekly meetings.
	18th	Facilitators Training – 20, mostly young people.
	20th	Census Team Training (1) – 10, all young people
August	12th	Census Team Training (2)
	16th	Maololo Meeting. 200+ attended. Water = Key Priority.
		Sub Village Census followed a week later.
	23rd	Women's Conference. 250+ attended.
September		
	6th and 7th	Leadership Workshop – 12 attended.
	11th	Maololo Second Meeting – women decide to take action.
	26th	Talane Meeting – start to build a new pre-school.
October	6th	Village Farewell Party for Manyaku/Trish.
	8th	Last Development Learning Group.

This starts in February and finishes in October 1997 – a snapshot in the development of the village of Mashabela. The last section headlines some developments that have taken place after 1997.

Nong Makola had been active in Mashabela village development for many years. He was invited to the fundraising training organised by the RWA in Apel in early 1997. I met him there the week after I first arrived from the UK, and again a month later. At the second workshop, we talked about my search for a suitable project for my research.

Mashabela was in the process of changing its village structure. The old tribal civic system (dominated by the Chief and his headmen) had been combined with a newer Development Forum (dominated by male village teachers) to create the Mashabela Development Council. All village committees (water, electricity, youth etc) and other groups such as the Traditional Healers and Burial Societies would be linked into one system and represented on the Council.

Mashabela appeared to have found a way of partnering 'traditionality' with development – on paper anyway. The Chief and the elders had agreed to work in development for the benefit of the village as a whole.

Nong, always keen to involve people in the life of his village, invited me to a meeting on 7th March to meet some of his village colleagues.

The First Development Workshop

At that first meeting, I offered to run a workshop for them. I was impressed by what I had seen and heard. I wanted them to see how I worked, so that they could decide if they wanted me to work with them further. In turn, I could decide if Mashabela would be suitable for my research. A planning group was formed to help shape the workshop. They agreed to my request, that at least half the participants in this and subsequent workshops or meetings would be women.

The planning group of three women and two men met on March 12th. Practical things were agreed. The women's garden group would provide tea and I would bring biscuits and two pots of strawberry jam. Bread would be bought on the day. Paulina, who was housekeeper to Father Patrick at the Catholic Mission, would be asked for help with facilities to make the tea. It was also decided to find someone to interpret at the workshop.

The planning group was not used to discussing things or working with a white woman, and the meeting was a lot more subdued than the previous one had been. A letter had been handed in from Phofogang, the garden women's group, suggesting that malnutrition, unemployment, literacy, and 'the controlling of a group' should be the focus of the workshop.

It was eventually agreed, in a manner of speaking, that the aims of the workshop would be to:

- involve people in village development matters;
- learn how to work together well; and
- build confidence that local people *can* contribute to developing their village.

During the meeting, Napé Diketani, one of the men, said, (White) 'People used to come and tell us what to do'. (Village) 'People must understand that we must plan for ourselves. They are not aware of this.'

The workshop took place on April 7th in Mashabela Primary School. A local head teacher called Willy Mashabela acted as interpreter. I borrowed a flipchart stand and paper from the RWA in Apel.

Mashabela Workshop – 7th April

Trish's Programme

9:15   Opening Prayer/Hymn

9:30   My Introduction
Who am I? Where from? Very brief. Arrangements for tea. Planning group aims for workshop up on flipchart. More than 50% women. Part of purpose of workshop to check me out. Help each other to be involved.

9:40   Introductions
Choose a symbol for your group that you like – draw it. Choose someone to introduce your group and symbol to everyone else.

10:00   Future Visioning
Imagine that the workshop is over! It was a great success. You all had a good time. What did you achieve? What are you saying? Share in pairs – then in group – FLIP ideas. Check with existing aims. Do they fit?

10:20   How Do Groups Work Well Together? (Groundrules)
Think of a successful meeting that you attended. Why was it good? What was happening? Write down some things that help people to work well together. Share. FLIP. This is how we will work together. OK?

10:45   Message To Mashabela Development Council

From what you have learnt now about people working together – Any messages that you want to give to MDC about how you want them to work?

Break

11:30   Vision

1. What are Mashabela's strengths? (abilities, positives, resources, feelings, opportunities) In small groups – record every one mentioned
2. What are the problems? (weaknesses, shortcomings, failings, threats) Record
3. What can you do – as local people – that would really make a difference to Mashabela? Record all your ideas. Reach for the sky!
4. Prioritise one idea/vision in your group.
5. Feedback

1:00   Endings – Closing Prayer/Hymn

---

16 women and 15 men attended the workshop.

5 small groups each prioritised a development vision for the village:

- **Africa Group** – 'To better our standard of living'

- **Farmers Group** – 'Empower ourselves'

- **Candle Grou**p – 'Train our groups'

- **Star Group** – 'Distribute water to each and every household'

- **Pen Group** – 'Planning'

The group process worked well. Many people arrived late but were able to join in and get involved. The timings of the programme were quite unrealistic, but this did not matter. The session eventually got going by mid morning and lasted most of the afternoon. The break needed a lot longer than was anticipated, to allow several trips to the Mission to make tea. None of the men made any move to help.

There was some lively discussion in many of the groups and the energy in the room was bright, active and open. It seemed that simply by taking part, men and women alike felt a sense of achievement. They left with smiles on their faces and even though for most of them, this was their first workshop, they had clearly enjoyed it.

One of the village elders later described the workshop as having 'inspired the people'. He may have said this to please – but the workshop was undoubtedly a success and the participants decided that they wanted me to work with them further in developing Mashabela.

The Development Learning Group

Things moved quickly after this.

Nong introduced me to the village and started to explain the life, history, and customs of Mashabela. We visited various parts of the village and met many different people. The 'village' was actually nine (sub) villages, with a combined population of well over 8,000 people scattered over a wide area. Some sub villages were much more connected and involved with the Development Council than others.

Nong and I started to meet regularly and decided to bring a small group together. The Learning Group, as it came to be known, would learn about the processes and principles involved in development, in order that they could facilitate village development themselves.

The Learning Group was recruited out of that first workshop, from people who had shown particular enthusiasm, contribution, and vision. People were chosen with a mix of ages, educational backgrounds, and sub-villages. Some of the men who might have been suitable were left out because of the commitment to ensure a majority of women. Two other men were invited, but withdrew after the first meeting, due to other commitments.

In the end there were 5/6 women:
    Alta Maroka*
    Annah Mashabela*
    Elizabeth Metwane
    Pinky Mashabela
    Terdla Mohuba*
and later
    Molefe Sello*

There were 4 men
    Libra Chumu*
    Napé Diketani*
    Nong Makola
    Richard Kgari

*Teachers

The Learning Group first met on 30th April. Just over half of the group were teachers, so the group was able to work in a mixture of Northern Sotho and English. We met most weeks in Mashabela Primary School near the Mission.

Learning Group Meeting Topics (April – October)

1. Coming together – discussing how we might work – developing our own opening and closing rituals – Sharing Vision for the Learning Group

2. How do we learn? Learning models that move away from teacher/student. What helps people to participate?

3. What is Development? (how to brainstorm) – Local people are the experts in the development of their own village.

4. 4 phases of development – Community Profile (collecting information and hard data) – Vision Building (collecting ideas from the village) – Action Plan (matching problems in profile with solutions from visions) – Implementation (Taking action). How can we take small 'actions' as we go?

5. Process and Outcome – what is a good process? How can we increase people's participation? Learning about trust through Learning Group Team Building

6. Collecting information > Zimbabwe village case study – profiling. What do funders/donors look for?

7. Planning model – using agriculture as metaphor for development intervention (spadework, fertilising/preparing soil, planting seeds, watering, harvesting). Planning 2nd village workshop. Personal values and group values and Village values.

8. Review process through review of 2nd village workshop. What went well? What didn't go well? What would we do differently another time? Planning the large village meeting – roles. Who does what? 'Everyone's idea is important' (an important value).

9. Power and elites – 'Putting the last first' (Chambers) – Who are last in Mashabela? How are they left out? Are we leaving them out? Maololo meeting planning.

10. The Tortoise and the Hare. Process and outcomes. Exclusion. Difference.

11. Women's Conference planning. Leadership workshop planning. Does love play a part in development?

12. Completion agenda (before Manyaku's departure). German Funders' Visit. Future planning (after Manyaku has left).

13. Learning Group review. What have we learnt? What has not gone well? What changes do we want to make? How will we say goodbye?

14. Last meeting with Manyaku. Goodbyes.

Attendance at Learning Group meetings was sometimes patchy and the meetings often started late. Pressing family matters took precedence for the women, but most people managed to come much of the time. The focus on learning enabled the group to reflect and discuss issues as they planned the village activities. They learned out of their own experience and from what they were actually doing in the village. I also introduced topics, which were important to include.

The Village Community Development Worker

For some time, Nong had been acting as unpaid village development worker through his role as chairperson of the Council. He was close to the old Chief and had helped to steer the new structure through the village mechanisms. However Nong's relationship with the women of the village was mixed; some of them were suspicious of him and did not altogether trust him. He had been out of work for some years and they were concerned that he was not reliable with money. These stories had been related to me early on, and I asked Nong directly about them. Partly as a result of this discussion, we were able to develop an honest and open relationship, which was tested during the months that followed.

We met regularly to reflect and make plans, which were then developed within the Learning Group. Nong was keen to learn all he could, and we worked on Nong's own ideas of his learning needs. I acted as mentor in this process. In turn, Nong offered a valuable source of information and understanding for my own learning about village development. In all aspects of development preparations, Nong was instrumental and very active in networking, encouraging and reminding people to come to workshops, meetings and village events. This role was a central and important one, without which much would simply have failed to happen.

When Nong was appointed as the village Community Development Worker, he resigned as chair of the village Executive Council. Nong was a member of the Learning Group.

Developments Gather Pace

The Learning Group decided to try to produce a development plan that would articulate the priorities in the village and hopefully support future funding. They were keen to involve as many village people as possible, so that the process itself would be rich in supporting local capacity. Women and young people's participation was prioritised. The Learning Group decided to focus on the nine sub villages, starting with Maololo, the most remote and probably the most disadvantaged.

Mashabela Development Plan

Sub Village Development – starting with Maololo

1. Sub Village Meeting/s – identifying development priorities

   - planned and run by sub village steering groups, which would include women and young people

   - involving gender and age-based small group discussions, supported by trained Facilitators

2. Population Information

   - collected by a trained Census Team

3. Development Action – on agreed development priorities

   - decided and undertaken by villagers themselves

Women's Conference

   - Planned and run by the women

   - With outside speakers

   - For the women only

Young People's Event

   - Planned and run by the young people themselves

The Village Development Plan

to be drawn from

   - Information collected from the census teams

   - Development Priorities agreed by the sub-villages at their meetings

   - Information And Priorities drawn from Council networks, the Women's Conference and the Young People's event

The village plan was taken to the Executive of Mashabela Council on 17th May and they agreed to go ahead with it. At the meeting, Nong was appointed Mashabela Community Development Worker (unpaid until funding could be found) and I was given formal permission to carry out my research in the village, in exchange for acting as consultant to the village for the development process. The Executive would continue to make the decisions whilst the Learning Group would facilitate the day to day process of village development.

All the Learning Group members attended this meeting, and enjoyed their new roles and developing leadership status in the village.

The Death of the Chief and the Second Development Workshop

On 14th June a village wide Cultural Day, to launch the new development structure, only attracted 20 people. On 20th June, the Chief died after a long illness – and the second workshop had to be postponed. Initially these events seemed to be considerable setbacks.

However, at the postponed second workshop, there appeared to be a stronger sense of village ownership for the development process. At the workshop, participants decided to run a village-wide meeting to involve the male elders and receive their blessing for the development plans. This was considered important, especially in the light of the death of the Chief.

2nd Mashabela Workshop (postponed) – 1st July

10:30   Prayer And Song
        Introductions And Welcome
        Goal – To prepare for the sub village process of
        1. consulting; 2. involving; 3. working together > Village Plan

10:45   Outline of Development Process – Manyaku – brief
        1. Experts in development are local people not outsiders.
        2. Working together to develop Mashabela
        Individual interest = me and mine. Collective = us = me + you + them

11:00   **What Do We Need To Live Well?** What is development all about?
        In groups of 5/6 (as sitting) – discuss all the things you need in Mashabela to LIVE…start from the most basic (shelter) and go on to include everything you can think of. Share – Feedback FLIP

11:45   Future Visioning

See the village as you want it. Imagine water etc. in place. Feel wet on your hands. Hear people talking about the developments. How does it feel? Any adjustments to your ideas?

Break

12:45   Sub Village Planning

Outline so far – See handout and work through in small groups
Share – Discuss – Questions – Decisions

1:15   Who Would Be Best For?

- Facilitators Team and when shall we train them?
- Census Team and People to collate information
- The Sub Village Leaders – to co-ordinate the sub village process

Feedback and **Discussion** and **Decisions**

1:45   Participation

- What helps you to work well together?
- Think of previous discussion – what helped you participate and what didn't?
- How does this affect the way decisions are made?

Feedback/Discussion. Pull out key principles – Participation

2:15   Endings – (Pull Together) – Song. Dance. Prayer.

Twenty-four people attended this second development workshop: 11 young people, 5 women, and 8 men. Some members of the Learning Group were unable to make it and the participants appeared to me to be less lively and bright than at the first workshop. However it was interesting that development as envisaged by the men focussed entirely on material and project outcomes, whilst the women and young people included qualities such as love, co-operation, and empowering leaders.

At a meeting of the Learning Group the following week, when the workshop was reviewed, members expressed considerable satisfaction with the outcomes. They were strongly behind the decision to hold a full Village Meeting, and had felt encouraged by the participation of the young people and the improved organisation of the refreshments. It was apparent that they were beginning to make connections between what they were learning and what they were experiencing in the village process.

Elizabeth said 'There is light for us now. We understand more now that we learn more. This light lets us see where we are going'.

The Chief was buried in Moshate on 5th July. It was a very important occasion for the village, and his funeral was attended by over a thousand village people and outside visitors. There was singing, dancing, and numerous speeches from visiting chiefs and others. Lunch was served to everyone after the funeral – a huge task, undertaken by the women from Moshate.

The Village Meeting

The Village Meeting took place four days after the funeral.

9th July

Nong joined me soon after I arrived. He seemed quite excited. I was surprised.

'There's no one here, Nong', I said to him, 'and the meeting is due to start in half an hour'.

I was still not yet used to the way that all meetings started late. This one had been announced at the Chief's funeral. There could be no better promotion opportunity. Hundreds of village people had been there. If they failed to respond, we would have to completely rethink.

Nong was undeterred. 'They are on their way', he said confidently. 'People are walking towards this place from all corners of the village'.

I loved the image this provoked and went over to one of the openings in the school courtyard to see for myself. I imagined crowds of people coming towards us – but when I looked out over the village; Mashabela looked much the same as ever.

'You may not be able to see yet', said Nong, who had come up beside me, 'but I promise you it is true. Many people are on their way. You will see' he said reassuringly.

Eventually people started to turn up and a brief pre-meeting was held to check out arrangements. Village meetings followed a prescribed format. It worked pretty well, giving a familiar structure that everyone understood. It was less successful in encouraging the women to participate and I was disappointed that none of the Learning Group women were there to run the meeting with the men, as we had planned. They had probably many pressing reasons – but I also knew that it was difficult for them to stand beside the men. This was not the way it was usually done.

A stream of people continued to arrive throughout the meeting, until the room was packed to bursting with well over 200 people. The older men had come first, some carrying gnarled walking sticks, the symbol of headmen. They came together or singly but never with the women. Large numbers of young people were also present. Plenty of women had turned up, but few said anything.

DJ, a teacher and member of the Executive, chaired the meeting skilfully, keeping things moving and ensuring that the purpose was never forgotten. Person after person, described the development plan and the proposals with increasing confidence and clarity

The excitement in the room built as one by one, people expressed support for different aspects of the plan. Many young people volunteered to be trained as facilitators and census team workers. Their numbers far exceeded our declared minimum. The women supported the idea of having their own conference, although they were reserved in how they showed this. A group would meet that afternoon, to start the planning. We smiled conspiratorially at each other across the room.

I congratulated Nong, DJ, Libra, Molefe and the others on the way they had run the meeting. We were all excited by the response of those at the meeting and Libra looked thrilled with the opportunity this would gave his precious Maololo. The village had given its blessing. We could go ahead.

The Facilitators and the Census Team Training

After the success of the village meeting, 20 people, mostly young, attended a one day facilitator's course. They received certificates at the Maololo meeting on 16th August.

Facilitators Training Plan – 18th July

1:00   **Prayer And Welcome, Introductions**
Purpose of training > Increasing Participation at meetings

1:20   **Development Plan Outline Review** – brief
Maololo Meeting   1) Hear needs of people (problems); 2) Hear ideas of people (solutions); 3) Take action together (later)
Facilitators make it **easy** ('facile' = word for easy in French) to participate

1:30   **Active Listening Exercise In pairs**
Feedback; Body Language; Eye contact; Confidence > all part of empowerment.

2:10   **Participation In small groups**
- Think about when you have felt nervous/shy in a meeting
- Think about when you have felt confident.
- What helps? What makes things worse?
Feedback – **Handout** on participation

2:30   **Maololo Meeting – 3 Key Questions** – Questions **Handout**

1. What do you love about living in Maololo?
2. What don't you like about living in Maololo? (problems etc.)
3. What could Maololo people do together that would really make a difference?

2:45   **Fish Bowl Exercise**

Three Groups enact the process that will run at Maololo

- Facilitator (3 observers to watch, observe, note – ask what is good here? What could be done to improve participation?) Question 1
- Change facilitator. (3 observers swop with 3 group members). Question 2
- Change facilitator. (Swop observers with group members). Question 3

Feedback

3:45   **Maololo Meeting Organisation**

Facilitators Role >>

- Organise people into small groups >> gender / age > Women. Men. Young People. Different groups in different rooms
- Set up 3 Questions > with Handouts.
- Try to have a literate person in each group to record (be sensitive about this)
- Circulate amongst your groups to :

    help them to stay on task with the questions;

    keep time; maximise participation

    encourage and praise and answer questions,

    ensure we are getting their ideas on paper.

    collect sheets of paper and give to DJ.

> Facilitators mixture of organisers, praise people, welcoming people, recorders.

4:00   **Review Day – Questions. Feedback**

4:30   **Prayer and Close.**

The facilitator's training was run in a mixture of Northern Sotho and English, and people participated well. They enjoyed themselves and there was plenty of laughter during the exercises. Feedback at the end suggested that they had made some useful connections from their own experience that extended their understanding of how to facilitate the participation of others.

Ten young people, who attended the facilitator's workshop, volunteered to be involved in the Census Team. They had their own training on 20th July and again on 12th August. Population information about Mashabela was non-existent and this was a good opportunity to gather basic information about the village.

The first census course was greatly oversubscribed and people whose English was limited were turned away. This was a difficult decision to make, running counter to previous training events, which were open to whoever wanted to attend.

Census Training Programme – 20th July and 16th August

10:30   Song and Prayer – Welcome and Introductions

10:50   Development Plan Outline – Meeting + Census + Action
The role of the census in the sub village process >> info about population.

11:00   Workshop Outline – interviewing skills + using the census questionnaire (see below)

11:10   Interviews
1. Establishing contact – Being polite, friendly and clear
2. Accomplishing the task – Being accurate – all doing the same
3. Finishing – Thanking and closing.

In pairs – Try out on each other. Pretend you are your own household and you are head of that household. Feedback Did you complete all task? Any difficulties?

11:40   Body Language – Role Play

12:00   Confidentiality and Respect
Basic value within development.
Keep confidence.

12:10   Dealing with Difficult Situations
In threes think of some situations that may occur that you may need help to deal with: Talk through.

12:30   Pilot Interviews
In pairs – find houses (preferably with people you don't know) and ask them to help you in your training by answering a few questions.

1:00   Feedback
Easy. Difficult. Problems. Confidence.

1:30   Collating Information
Each pair in turn fill in large chart from responses.

2:00   Census Team Organisation
Choose leaders. Arrange when and who and how

Review and Close

The census training also went well after the initial hiccup – although the second day had to be rescheduled when no-one turned up. When it took place, the participants especially enjoyed the role playing. They became quite playful and the session was amusing and funny. They said that they had learnt about relating to others in ways they had not considered before. They chose Marumo Makau, a young teacher from Maololo, as their team leader. A few weeks later, he did a great job of organising the Maololo census and collating the information that was collected.

Participants on both training courses received attendance certificates at the Maololo Meeting.

The Maololo Meeting

On 16th August, over two hundred people gathered in Maololo for the first sub village meeting.

16th August

It was extraordinary to see all the children left standing under the tree. How could we have forgotten them?! There were so many of them...

After the opening formalities in the school yard, everyone had gone happily into their separate classrooms to discuss the development questions in small groups, shepherded along by the facilitators. Everyone seemed highly organised and well prepared. I suspected that the questions had already been discussed in the village for days.

I went over to talk to Napé, when Elizabeth came up to us. 'What shall we do with the children?' she asked. We turned round and there, under the tree, stood over one hundred children all under 11 years old, grinning expectantly at us.

Napé was quite unmoved and announced that he would facilitate them himself in one large group. Elizabeth offered to help him and the two of them started explaining the questions to the children, who immediately shouted out their answers with gusto.

Later, after everyone had re-gathered outside, it was announced that every group, including the children had prioritised safe water. This was no surprise. Maololo's wells were horribly polluted, since they were shared with the animals. We agreed to reconvene within the month, bringing a water engineer to offer advice to them.

Delighted Maololo people streamed out of the schoolyard. They had loved the attention on their village. It was a new experience for them. One person told me that he felt as if his village had been 'brought in' to Mashabela. Libra was overjoyed. Over 200 people had attended the meeting – 42 women, 48 young people, 10 men and 110 children. After the census team had done their work, we worked out this represented over 50% of the entire population of Maololo, which included the men who worked away.

A month later, we returned with Bob, an experienced water engineer, as promised. We met in one of the classrooms – a much smaller group than before. He explained the options. They could dig out a well themselves, but it was dangerous unless they lined it with cement rings, which would cost money. The other option was to wait for the government to sink a bore hole, but Bob explained that the chance of finding water in this area, with this rock structure, was poor. They might have to wait for a long time.

A long discussion followed. From the mood in the room, I really thought that they would decide to wait for the government to act. But I was wrong.

After a long pause, a woman at the back shouted something – and the rest cheered loudly. They had decided to dig out one of their wells themselves and fence it off from the animals. 'When can we start?' they asked.

It was a moment of real drama. Even Bob looked surprised. Having worked in the area for a long time, he was used to village people wanting things done for them, not doing them for themselves. He promised to get back quickly with costs and arrangements.

The Maololo process was a highpoint for the Learning Group, and considered a great success by everyone involved. Other sub villages were slow in following Maololo's example and getting their meetings underway.

Talane, a large sub village close to the tarred road, held a meeting amongst themselves without the support either of the facilitators or census team. They decided to go ahead and build a new pre-school that would house up to 30 children, next to an old corrugated iron building that was currently used. They raised enough funds through a house to house collection, to buy breeze blocks to build the foundations and start the walls. On 26th September, I was invited to photograph the laying of the first wall. The pre-school building was finished 12 months later.

The Women's Conference

This turned out to be one of the most difficult but arguably the most productive developments of the period. From the start, the women planned, funded, and organised the conference themselves. At the weekly planning meetings, more and more women got involved. The planning process itself involved the women in ways that they were quite new to them. It also developed the confidence, creativity, and leadership of the small group of women who were chosen by the women, as their leaders. Several of these were members of the Learning Group. The weekly meetings were held in the Tribal office without any men present – an unheard of happening – and the women funded the conference themselves through a house to house collection.

The day was a great success. It was the first Women's Conference ever held in Mashabela or in the surrounding area, and the message to village women about the value of their participation came through loud and clear.

23rd August

I was visiting an NGO in Pietersburg (now Polokwane) to ask them if they could provide a speaker for the conference. The woman agreed, providing her husband came too. 'Oh no, I am sorry', I said. 'It is for women only'. She looked surprised. In South Africa, men attended women's conferences too, she said.

I was shocked. Had I imposed this women-only rule on Mashabela – or had the women decided it themselves? I couldn't remember how it had developed. I had certainly assumed that a Women's Conference would be just for women. It would be at home – but things here in rural South Africa were obviously different.

Before coming out to South Africa, I had attended a conference in Sheffield about 'Afrocentricity in Research'. A leading African American, Professor Asante had spoken about the importance of putting Africa at the centre of research with African people – rather than blindly following a Eurocentric approach. I had tried hard to be aware of this in Mashabela by explicitly showing my respect for their culture and being as mindful as I could about my assumptions. But I was not confident that I was always as aware as I would wish to be.

The following day, just three days before the conference, we had our last Learning Group meeting to tidy up last loose ends. MJ, DJ and some other members of the Executive of the village Council had joined us.

A number of worrying developments had emerged. A male staff member of the RWA, which ran the women's gardens, had told the women to keep away from the conference and not to donate their vegetables. The implied threat was unmistakable and the garden women were alarmed and fearful and said that they definitely would not be coming. This put Altah and Elizabeth, both members of the gardens and the Learning Group, in a very difficult position.

In addition to this, there was a story, from the same source, that Nong and I had misappropriated some funds. It was a ridiculous tale and wholly untrue. I said I thought the women's response was much more serious and we could ignore the other story.

Nong did not agree. He was clearly upset. He announced that he and the men felt they should attend the conference, in order to support the women to manage the situation. Many outside agencies were coming. The difficulties were very serious. The women, he said, had no experience of running anything of this size or complexity.

My heart sank and I could feel myself becoming both alarmed and irritated. I turned to the women, realising how important it was for me not to react or intervene. They must decide what they wanted to do. It was an important moment. Would they acquiesce to the men?

Altah, Elizabeth and Molefe sat with completely implacable expressions. I marvelled at their apparent lack of reaction. 'We will be ok', they said quietly, one by one. Their message was clear. The men should keep away.

The following day, Nong and I met under Mashabela Primary school tree. He was quite specific. 'They are not up to it' he said, clearly feeling things very intensely. I reflected soberly that this was probably the highest profile development event ever organised in Mashabela. He was being excluded. Even though I felt very frustrated with him, I also had some sympathy for his position.

We had a strong exchange and I couldn't help but be impressed by his challenge. He had acquired status by bringing me into the village and he was risking losing it, by challenging me in this way. I thought I sensed some sadness under his anger, but both of us were passionate about our own position. I was insistent that he and the men should keep away. He was convinced they should be there.

I felt quite troubled by the whole situation but if I withdrew from my position with Nong, I felt sure that he and the other men would override the women.

Saturday dawned and I woke with some foreboding. I had not slept well and had had a difficult day, the day before, shopping in Pietersburg with Julia, one of the conference organisers. We had gone into town to buy food for the conference and I was concerned that we didn't have enough. The vegetables donated from the women's gardens would have saved the day.

Julia was unperturbed and with the boot full of a sack of maize meal, cabbages and bags from the supermarkets, she was intent on finding chickens to finish off her shopping. I had not thought things through at all, when she shouted for me to stop a few miles out of Pietersburg, but still a long way from Mashabela.

She proceeded to barter with a woman at the farm stall and with great glee announced that she had bought 13 chickens at a bargain price. Slowly it dawned on me that there was no where else for the chickens except inside the car, alive and squawking. What followed is not for telling here – but as we drove down the road back to Mashabela, with chicken feathers blowing all over the car, I was aware that this was going to make a great story when I got home. I longed to be finished with the experience and doing the telling!

By the time the conference was due to start, there were precisely ten people present. There were four outside speakers, including a powerful looking woman from the ANC Women's League, a small group of RWA workers, Altah and Elizabeth, looking very fine in their traditional dresses, and me. By now, I was used to events starting late, but somehow I had imagined that the conference would be different. I was wrong.

Four hours later, the large schoolroom was packed to capacity and lit up with joy, noise and excitement. Hundreds of women of all ages were crammed inside and many others outside, were peering in through the cracked and broken windows. Village funerals had delayed them, but women continued to come and go all through the afternoon

Altah was 'MC' for the day and despite having never done it before, she was brilliant, leading the women in singing and dancing, and introducing each speaker. Everyone was fed – a small miracle, assisted by the RWA, who having stopped the garden women from helping, turned up with large sacks of vegetables and largesse from Apel.

Nong and MJ had appeared at the edge of the courtyard just before things got started. Terdla went over to speak to them and reported impassively that they said that they were there to check that we were ok. To my considerable relief, they left soon after.

Later in the afternoon, on venturing out of the school reluctantly, to use one of the pit latrines nearby, I came across Magogodi, a young man I knew quite well from the workshops. He greeted me excitedly and asked if the women were plotting against the men. 'Will it be ok?' he asked. I did not know,

I told him – but the women were having a great time and as far as I could tell, the men were far from their minds. He walked off looking confused!

The woman from the ANC Women's League gave a rousing speech, encouraging the women to realise the value and power of their participation. Red guava trees were given to raffle ticket winners, the speakers and those who had organised the conference. I gave one to Segapi Makola, Nong's wife in front of everyone.

At the end of the day as the sun was sinking rapidly, I gave Altah and Elizabeth a lift home. On the way we saw several women walking back along the road with guava trees on their heads. 'Thank God it is over', said Elizabeth. It was the only remark I ever heard any of them make, in reference to the difficulties we had experienced. I had to agree!

The Women's Conference Postscript

I met with Nong at the Tribal Office the following Tuesday. He was rather quiet but we got through our work together. I asked him if he had heard any reports of the conference. He said that his wife was very proud of her tree and that the women seemed pleased with how things had gone. He wanted to hear about the speakers and I passed him a copy of my speech in which I had mentioned his work and my belief in the importance of working in partnership with the men. He made no comment.

We got up to go to a meeting on the other side of the village. On impulse, I slipped my hand through his arm, as we walked across the yard to the car. I could feel the joy and relief running through him. We said nothing but I knew we had made up our fight.

Many weeks later when I interviewed Nong as part of my research, we discussed what had happened. 'I thought nothing would ever be the same again' he said solemnly.

Others commented on our argument. They were impressed that we had resolved things so quickly. This was unusual in their culture, where arguments could last for generations. Many told me that my disagreement with Nong and the way we made up had been talked about with interest in the village.

The outcomes of the women's conference continued to evolve. The men's fears evaporated in the days and weeks that followed. No revolution was forthcoming. This was not Mashabela women's style. The changes were quite subtle – but definite. The women had learnt that they could do things on their own without the men, and that their participation was important. They were more confident, and this showed in their participation at village meetings.

The Leadership Workshop

Some of the teachers who worked out of the village, asked for their own training workshop. The Learning Group decided to support this, and it was arranged to run a Leadership Workshop in Nkgonyeletse High School over the weekend of 6th and 7th September.

It was rather an experiment in a number of ways. Recruitment was through invitation, involving people with reasonable English who had a leadership role. Lunch was organised, which participants were asked to pay for. This was not popular and it became hard to find people to participate. The teachers who had originally expressed interest did not materialise, and it was difficult to recruit women, who were reluctant to come forward.

In the end, however, 12 people attended, including the nursing sister from the Clinic, the secondary school head teacher, several members of the Learning Group (all men), a few other teachers, and a couple of younger women, who had taken on organising roles in the women's conference. There were more men than women and the meals ran at a loss and had to be subsidised.

The high point of the workshop was the visit of Peter Anderson, Head Teacher of St Mark's College (an independent school for Sekhukhuneland children). He was highly respected in the locality, and his visit was considered a great honour for Mashabela.

Leadership Workshop

6th and 7th September

10:00   Introductions and Goals

10:45   Outline

10:50   **Workshop Groundrules** (using cards on a wall) (challenge/safety)

11:10   **Leaders and their Style** – Autocratic, Democratic, Laissez Faire

11:25   **My Leadership** (pairs) – What is your style? How do you lead?

12:00   **Being Led** – What can I learn from being led? positive/difficult experiences

12:30   *Lunch*

1:30   **Warm Up** (music)

1:45   **Proactive – Reactive**. Making plans and Staying on track

2:00	Peter Anderson Visit
2:30	Questions and Discussion
4:00	Plans for Tomorrow

Sunday

10:00 Carousel

1. Who is the leader you admire most and why?
2. What did you learn from Peter Anderson's visit yesterday?
3. What are you enjoying about this workshop?

10:15 Grounding

Being grounded is being balanced and centred = aware of sensations 'inside' and 'outside' using your 5 senses. Present in the Here and Now

11:00 Mirroring in Pairs

Leading and Following. Feedback

11:30 Self, Others And Context – information you need to be a good leader – from yourself; from others; from context

12:30 *Lunch*

1:30 Dance – Being Aware, inside and outside, around you.

2:15 Goal Setting. Concentrate on what you want.

3:20 Review

Leaders and their styles, Peter Anderson, Proactive/Reactive, Self, Others, Context, Grounding, Goal Setting

3:50 Personal Plan (solo)

Three things I have learnt and want to apply – actions – support to stay on track.

4:00 Go Round. Feedback one highlight and one action

4:30 Close and **Hymn** and **Prayer**

6th and 7th September

The Leadership Workshop

The peace of our workshop was broken as thunder crashed outside and rain started to hammer down onto the corrugated iron roof of the classroom. The noise was incredible. It quickly got dark and of course, there were no lights to turn on. The roof was no match for the onslaught of rain and it soon started to leak in several places. It was impossible to hear anything over the din.

We walked to the windows, smiling at each other, and watched the rain dance in the rapidly forming puddles. It was early for the summer rains and the ground was very dry. I vaguely wondered how I would manage the thirty kilometres of dirt track, home to Apel.

MJ shouted at me 'God is blessing our workshop!' I smiled at him, liking the image. Rain was very precious here – so different from the UK, where we invariably complain when there is a downpour.

We were nearing the end of our second day. The workshop had been a bit of a departure. I had felt uncomfortable about running it exclusively for the teachers, who were already a powerful elite – but we decided to go ahead, in the hope that they would learn something about leadership, finding ways to empower others. In the end, several non-teachers had come too.

I brought a portable CD player with me with a selection of African music. Two full days was much longer than the other village workshops I had run. Breaks would be important.

There were very varying levels of confidence in the group. You could see the women hanging back and letting the men monopolise discussions. One of the younger women, called Monkie, hung her head whenever I looked at her, yet we knew each other quite well from the women's conference. She only acted coyly when men were present. It was depressing to realise how much would need to change, for things to be different for the women.

After a bit, I turned on the music and everyone stood up smiling, not needing any encouragement to dance. There was no self-consciousness. The sun shafted through the side windows changing their moving figures into dark profiles dancing in millions of highlighted specks of dust – poignantly beautiful and graceful. I was very moved by the image.

This little interlude was typical of how the workshop had developed. We had periods of intense work, learning about ourselves – followed by lighter more informal times, when we danced or shared stories.

The rain stopped and the sun came out again. Our workshop was finished. We stood in a circle, with Monkie, leading us in a hymn, her voice soaring beautifully over the harmonies of the others. We walked out into the sunlit courtyard, now damp and fresh from the rain.

The German Donors' Visit

On the 17th September, three German donors, who were visiting the RWA in Apel, came to spend the day in Mashabela. They had responsibility for a small development fund in Germany. The village hoped that they might be interested in supporting their development plans.

An itinerary had been arranged, which included a trip to Maololo. Several people from the Learning Group, the Executive Committee, and some young people were involved in explaining different aspects of the proposals to them.

The visit was a challenge to organise. It mostly fell to Nong to arrange. Mashabela Council had no funds to buy food and drink for this sort of event. In the end some money was found and the women from Moshate did the cooking.

The visit went smoothly, and the Germans were given documents outlining the village development plan. To Mashabela, they were white and therefore rich – so their visit attracted a lot of interest. Molefe, the newest and youngest member of the Learning Group, commented that 'white men in our village is a sign that we are well known now'.

The visit finished in the Tribal Offices at Moshate, where Nong gave a speech. At the end he said:

'Our people have inherited the habit of being externally driven. They have been taught that they are no good at managing...that they are incompetent...that they cannot do anything on their own...Please fund Mashabela...(to) build capacity, improve skills and enable us to start projects like our Community Farming.'

Reviews, Farewell and New Starts

On 6th October, the village threw me a farewell party in Nkgonyeleste High School.

As a result of the development activity and some regional networking by the Learning Group, a number of outside agencies had recently become involved in Mashabela. The party was an opportunity for them to explain their work.

A Health Department officer from Jane Furse spoke about a Sanitation Project, which would be starting shortly. There would be jobs for village people in the building of the VIPs (Ventilated Improved Pit latrines) for those who could afford the subsidised fee.

A worker from Tlhavhama Training Initiative, an NGO in Pietersburg, spoke about work he had started with Mashabela Development Council, designing a legal constitution. Mashabela had just joined Tlhavhama, and some members of the Learning Group and Executive Committee were starting to attend their training events. This was to prove an important resource for Mashabela, and would continue the process of developing skills, confidence, knowledge, and capacity within the village.

Bob Cousins, from Tsaogang, spoke about the Water Feasibility Study, which was to collect information about village water sources, quality, and population needs. It would be a first step to funding a village water system. This was welcome news.

Another Health Department official was there to report on the progress of the new Clinic building. He anticipated that it would be operational before the end of the following year, and explained that doctors would visit from Jane Furse hospital to hold regular weekly surgeries for the first time in Mashabela.

In addition to this, Executive Committee members reported that they had had a meeting with Eskom to press them to supply electricity to the village, and a visit to Telkom was planned to ask them to install a public telephone at Mpanama cross in the centre of the village.

Temperatures soared in the schoolroom as the afternoon heat built. I made a brief report to the Executive Committee with some recommendations about future priorities.

Report To The Executive Committee Mashabela Development Council

By Trish Bartley (aka Manyaku)
6th October

1. **Developments Undertaken Since April.**
   - The Learning Group
   - 3 Workshops – Vision building; Planning; Leadership Building
   - Community Development Worker (Nong Makola) training and development
   - Sub Village process – including Facilitators and Census training – Maololo and Talane
   - Women's Conference
   - Fundraising – Outline Proposal, German visitors, Mvula connection.
   - Research Interviews (June and September)
   - Networking – Tlhavhama; Mvula; Tsaogang; Operation Hunger; Tlhatlholanang; Rural Development Forum; Department of Health; Department of Environmental Health.

2. **Recommendations** – To:
   a) Complete and prioritise Financial Management Systems and Constitution work
   b) Support the sub village process – Meetings, Census, Action (see information sheet)
   c) Continue with:
   Monthly report from Community Development Worker
   Monthly report from Learning Group
   Regular village meetings to keep everyone involved
   e) Make plans and stick to them unless you make a decision to do otherwise.
   f) Consider employing Ana Agostino (Johnston St., Pretoria 0132), to write up your Development Plan to your instructions at the end of the sub village process (R3,000)

3. **Acknowledgements and Thanks to**
   Moshate – especially Hunadi and Mtladi – and Phaaphle, for my name.
   The Learning Group and especially Nong Makola, for all his hard work
   The Women of Mashabela
   RWA and Sister Mary for my accommodation, support and funding help
   Father Patrick Gallagher
   Many other Mashabela people who have made me welcome

I gave trees to members of Moshate and each of the sub villages and to members of the Learning Group and Executive Committee.

The following day, the Learning Group met for the last time. I gave them each a file, which contained handouts and notes of the work we had done together. Six weeks earlier, the Learning Group had undertaken a review and looked at the changes they wanted to make.

The Learning Group Review – 13th August

Elizabeth, Napé, Libra, Altah, Richard, Nong, (Pinky apols) Manyaku.

What Have We Gained/Learnt? (positives)

- Self Confidence and Leadership
- Evaluation / Review methods
- Planning > Gold [goal?] Setting
- Principles of Development
- Friendship
- Vision Building
- Sub Village Process
- Values

What Has Not Gone So Well? (negatives)

- Withdrawal of some members at the beginning
- Not included a member of Moshate in the LG
- Neglected to develop youth leadership

What Changes Do We Want To Make To The Learning Group? (changes)

- New LG members from Mahlakanaseleng – Molefe (Alta to invite) – Magogodi (Nong to say that we would have liked to invite him if school not more important) and Boche (Libra to invite back into the group)
- In October, when the Learning Group will need to re-form after Manyaku's departure, other people will also be invited – Marumo Makau and Patrick Makgwale from Maololo and others as thought best
- Need to consider how LG can best support youth leadership in the village
- Decide to ask Phaahle to appoint someone from Moshate to join the LG immediately

How shall we end this phase of the Learning Group and plan for the future?

- Plan a shared meal in the mission to celebrate and say goodbye?
- Look at the future of the LG – consider a name change – how the group will work together after October.

Later in 1997

Village Sanitation Project. Local people employed.

Trial bore hole drilled in Maololo – large water source found

Village water feasibility study started

New Health Clinic opened

Co-operative Farmland Project started

1999

Clinic and Mission electrified

2000

March 20th – May 9th
Trish returned to Mashabela to evaluate research

2001

Village Water System (taps in the road). 75% of village covered. Maololo and Ga Selepe still waiting for their system

Village electrification. 50% village. Maololo and other distant areas not covered.

Moshate announces intention to take over Mission land. Land Reform NGO involved in negotiations.

Area Sports facilities being built at Apel Cross

Community water management study starts

2002

German donors return to offer funding for poultry projects

New developments were now in hand and things were changing fast. There were many dates for meetings scheduled. It was unclear what the role of the Learning Group would be in this new phase – or if it had one at all. Altah and Elizabeth had been co-opted onto the Executive Committee of the Council to join Napé, Libra and Richard, who were already members. Molefe was active in the water committee. Women were involved in village meetings and committees and in their gardens and resource centre. It was hoped that the learning of group members would benefit the village, wherever they were involved.

The Developments That Followed

The flurry of activity with outside agencies that started at the end of 1997 gradually subsided.

The sanitation project was successfully completed. A number of new pit latrines were built, and, importantly, a few local jobs were created for a few months. This had a significant if temporary impact on local livelihoods.

Over the next twelve months, local people established an ANC branch in the village, which may have helped improve relationships with the Transitional Local Council. In 1999 they agreed to fund a village water system. Consultants were appointed and by 2001 most village households (in the centre of the village) had access to water from taps in the roads.

Maololo, however, was not included in these plans – nor was Ga Selepe. Nearly five years after their decision to dig out their well, they were still drinking polluted water. It is said that funding has been allocated to provide them with their own water system, but I know no definite news.

Back in November 1997, as a result of his contact with Maololo, Bob Cousins, the water engineer, brought a professor from Pretoria to survey the land around Maololo. To everyone's surprise, a trial bore hole found a very large volume of water. At first it was believed to be so extensive that there was talk of this water supplying the whole of Mashabela. People involved in the new Farmland Co-operative Project, initiated by Nong Makola, wondered whether they might even get their fields irrigated. Months and years have passed, and as far as I know, nothing further has happened. Maololo is a very remote area, and a bridge and road would need to be built in order to develop the bore hole.

As is always the case, the areas furthest away from the centre are developed last. When funding is limited, developments are provided for the most number of people. This results in villages like Maololo being left out and disadvantaged.

Other news is better. Slightly over 50% of the village is now electrified, and a village telephone has at last been installed at Mpanama Cross. Village committees were busy in negotiating these developments with the authorities. Electricity will make a great difference to the village, although the cost will be too great for many families to afford.

Football has blossomed, and a new sand pitch with a spectator area, close to the main road, has been developed. A few miles north, at Apel Cross, a government scheme is building a sports centre.

The young queen Hunadi was crowned in 1998 and members of Mashabela Council worked hard to get her accepted as chief by the authorities and everyone in the village. Hunadi has since given birth to two children – both girls – and lives in Moshate in a new house built for her by the village.

The women's appointments on the Executive Committee did not endure. They found it hard to attend meetings, with all their other commitments, and did not feel comfortable in their new positions alongside the men. However, they continue to be very active and effective in leading the women in the gardens and in the women's resource centre. Some people from Ireland, staying in the Mission, have helped to irrigate the women's gardens.

The Learning Group never met again. Nong Makola received a salary from the Tribal Office for his work as Community Development Worker for a short time. Then funds became short and the young queen Hunadi was crowned. The old order changed and the Development Council was told to move out of the Tribal Office.

The new Clinic was opened in 1998, and as promised, doctors regularly visit to treat local people. The village Health Committee, chaired by D.J. Makau, organised a fine opening event, which was attended by local dignitaries.

Since then, HIV infection has soared, and according to current projected statistics up to 30% of the working population may die by 2006. A group of young people is working hard to hold training events to promote the important message of safer sex – but tragically, it will be too little and too late to save many lives.

Mashabela, as with other rural areas, is changing rapidly. In the next 5-10 years, HIV/AIDS will decimate the population, affecting young people and women the worst. There are many orphaned children being cared for by grandmothers. It is hard to imagine how villages like Mashabela will come though.

'On the hardest rocks, sometimes you see beautiful flowers growing'.[2]

Appendix 1

Mashabela Development Plan –
Sub Village Process Proposed Outline Budget

September 1997	R
Action funding for each sub village (xR4,000) not including Maololo	32,000
Maololo funding for digging out 2 wells (cost of cement rings, technical help, fencing, well lids, hand pumps) (all labour free from within Maololo)	18,000
Transport costs for 1000 trees per sub village (trees available for free)	4500
Publicity and photocopying (30c a sheet) Census interview sheets >1 per household, posters, programs, letters etc.	1000
Transport (R20 per one way journey to Pietersburg) (all photocopying, cheap shopping, banking and networking in Pietersburg) (this allows 2 people x 2 return journeys per fortnight)	2080
Financial and other capacity building training (both 'tailor made' for MDC and participating in outside training courses)	3000
Financial Audit, stationery, postage and telephone and other office expenses	2500
Refreshments for village meetings (tea and bread) (and for census team)	800
Consultant fees for co-ordinating the village development plan from all 9 sub village meetings, census information and any development weekend outcomes	3000
Typing and photocopying the plan	500
Brick Project start up funding (cost of materials and training)	2000
Total	**R 69,380** **(£9,000 in 1997)**

Appendix 2

Mashabela Development Network September 1997

Executive Committee

Chairperson	Mr Malegodi. Richard Kgari
Vicechair	Mr M.J. Makanatleng
Secretary	Mrs. Hunadi Alta Maroka
Assistant Secretary	Mr Ditonkana Libra Chumu
Treasurer	Mrs. Elizabeth Metwane
Project Co-Ordinator	Mr Dithopi J. Makau
	Mrs Paulinah Sello
	Mrs Mokgebeleko Makgony
	Mr Napé J. Diketani
	Mr Makatane Malesa
CD Worker	Mr Nong John Makola
Ex Officio/Moshate	Mr Masegotji Joseph Mashabela

The Learning Group

Annah Mashabela

Elizabeth Metwane

Pinky Malegwale

Napé Diketani

Nong Makola

Alta Maroka

Molefe Sello

Terdla Mohuba

Libra Chumu

Richard Kgari

Census Teams

Team 1

Marumo Makau – Maololo

Regina Maroka – Mahlakanaseleng

Welheminah Diketani – Mapulani

Marema Sello – Maololo

Maepe Makau – Maololo

Donald Diketani – Maololo

Team 2

Magogodi Mashabela – Malegasane

Monkie Mashabela – Malegasane

Molefe Sello – Mahlakanaseleng

Betty Mongwai – Mohwelere

Selepe Legasa – Ga Selepe

Soweto Diphofa – Mapulane

Facilitators Team

D.J. Makau – Maololo

Bosoaneng – Maololo

M.M. Makau – Maololo

M.J. Makanatleng – Talane

R.L. Selepe – Ga Selepe

*M.M. Sello – Mahlakaseleng

Stephinau Makau – Maololo

Kgoroshi L Malatje – Ga Selepe

*Monica Sello – Malegasane

*Linda Makau – Maololo

*Ramatsemele Monkie Mashabela – Malegasane

Makgwale Makhulwane Phillip – Malegasane

Napé Diketani – Mahlakanaseleng

Soweto Diphofo – Talane

*Mogwai Matlale B – Mohwelere

*Eldah Melodi – Malegasane

*Matwampe Julia Mashabela – Malegasane

Magogodi Mashabela – Malagasane

Letsau Malegodi Anthony – Malegasane

*Ina Sello – Mahlakanaseleng

* Women

Appendix 3

HOUSE NUMBER

MALE/FEMALE

CENSUS QUESTIONNAIRE
MAOLOLO SUB VILLAGE
week of 18th August

Speaking in N. Sotho

I am working on behalf of the Mashabela Development Council. This is my letter of authorisation. We are conducting a POPULATION CENSUS to help us collect the information we need to develop the village.

1.   Are you willing, to answer a few questions about your household and who lives here with you?
      YES / NO

2.   Are you the head of this household YES/NO   **If No   >>**
      Is it possible to speak to the head of this household?   **If No >>**
                                Please can I interview you?

3.   How many people live permanently in your household ?

4.   How many children under 7 live here?

5.   How many young people between 7 - 21 live here ?

6.   How many adults over 21 live here (including yourself)

                                                        Check the totals - Do 4+5+6 = 3

6a   How many of these are men?

6b   How many are women ?   *Check the totals - Do 6a + 6b = 6?*

7.   Are any members of your household working away?

7a   How many?

7b   Did you include them in the adult numbers above?

Thank you very much for your help with this questionnaire.

Have you written house number at top of page?   Have you written M / F in top box?

COMMENTS OVER PAGE - Conversations - Concerns - Questions.

Appendix 4

Maololo Meeting Programme

August 16 – 10:00 hours
Mamorithing Primary School

1. M.C.	Libra Chumu
2. Prayer	Mr Abram Makgwale/ Mmakau Lefolwane
3. Welcome	Mrs Paulina Sello
4. Introduction of Guest	Sello Andries
5. The Sub Village Development Process	Nong J. Makola
6. Maololo Village	Libra Chumu
7. Maololo Women	Magdeline Makau
8. Maololo Youth	Makgwale Patrick
9. Mashabela Development Council	Kgari M.R.
10. The Role of the Learning Group	Mrs Alta Maroka
11. Maololo Census	Marumo Makau
12. Guest Speaker	Manyaku
13. Small Group Discussions – in the school	
14. Feedback From the Small Groups	Facilitator's Team
15. Decision About Focus of Maololo Development	D.J. Makau
16. Question and Answers	N.J. Makola
17. Vote of Thanks	D.J. Makau
18. Announcements	
19. Closure and Prayers	Abram/Lefolwane

Napé Diketani

My full name is Napé Johannes Diketani. I am 41 years old and am married with a daughter of 19 years and a son of 10 years old.

When my father was alive, I lived here in Mashabela – though my wife lives in the Orange Free State and my children are at school in Johannesburg and Pretoria.

In 1997, I worked on MDC executive as Deputy Chairperson and I was also Chairperson of the Pastoral Council of my Church (Catholic) – and a leader of my sub village committee. I was a member of the Development Learning Group and used to translate for Manyaku at meetings.

I think I have changed. I used to argue, especially in meetings, but now, because I'm more involved in development, I only agree. If I notice I've hurt somebody, I say 'Sorry my brother' or 'Sorry, my sister'. But some years back, I'd say 'Oh to hell with him'!

Even when I am sure that what I am saying is correct – I usually use the words 'I am suggesting this' — to open a room for discussion. I was tempted to say 'I am saying this' – but that sounds like instructing and if they don't like it and say 'no', I feel hurt.

A leader who instructs people will get a lot of confrontation. People will oppose him. The leader will think that they are undermining him, whilst the people might say that this is good, and this is not good. But an enlightened leader will always use strategies and tactics to empower people. He wants their ideas to come through.

In a workshop or a meeting, I try to talk a little so that others can talk a lot. If you try to empower others but at the same time you dominate, it is no good.

In development, we do not work with the intention of scoring points. We are there to develop everyone. We are not there to undermine anyone's idea, unlike in politics. For example in the ANC, we are saying this. In the PAC, we are saying that. In development we accept ideas. But in politics no, we select. In politics we argue!

In the past we were going in one direction, and others in another. Now we have our goal, which is our development. If everyone is involved, the process is easier. If some are not involved, we might feel as if we are working in two groups – those who understand and those who do not. We might end up at loggerheads. When everybody understands, we can explain that some aims cannot be achieved in one day. They might take years.

Development is often seen as projects – getting water, electricity or this or that, or getting money. We must start by developing people. Then it will be easier for them to organise themselves, so that they can prioritise things and work on the basic needs of their community. Needs will differ in each village.

When people are developed, it is easier for them to do things gently – do things as a team.

We were right to concentrate on learning. Learning doesn't have limitations. One cannot say I have learned up to here and it is enough.

I remember the togetherness in our learning. You know, in our culture, it is not easy for a man to mix with a woman. But through the Learning Group, it became easy. We got used to treating each other as brothers and sisters.

When a village is united we see progress. In meetings that are convened by the Chief, if there is something that dissatisfies us, we have got the power to speak out. But if the village is not united, we have a way of ignoring things. We are afraid to say 'This is not right'.

A villager might say 'yes, Sister Mary is a good developer', because they can see the gardens and the women's centre projects. In the case of Manyaku, they can say that she has done nothing, because she has left this place still dry.

But it will depend on the individual. The Learning Group would not say that. Sister Mary was here for many years. Manyaku was here for some months.

When we give someone a fish to eat – we just say take this and eat. But when that fish is finished, we'll just wait for someone to come along with another fish. But if you show us where you got that fish, so that even in your absence we can go to the dam – to try to get the fish – then it will be easier for us to survive, even in your absence. Don't make it that we can survive only in your presence. We become so embarrassed.

My message to people about development is:

'We do not want to depend on others, we want to develop ourselves and stand on our own. At the end of the day you must not say so and so has done this for us – you must say WE – we have done this'.

THREE

The Learning

In order to arrive at what you do not know
You must go by a way which is the way of ignorance.
In order to possess what you do not possess
You must go by the way of dispossession.
In order to arrive at what you are not
You must go through the way in which you are not.
And what you do not know is the only thing you know
And what you own is what you do not own
And where you are is where you are not.

From *The Four Quartets*, T.S. Eliot[1]

The purpose of this chapter is to share the learning that came out of the Mashabela development – by discussing and evaluating the stages of the intervention, exploring the qualities of love, power ,and learning that framed the research, and sharing some models and theories that have influenced me. Within a context that suggests that there is no one right way of working and many wrong ways – I point out a few signposts that are important guides for me on my path of practice.

In the mutual process of development, in which local people and practitioners can learn with and from each other, I have often been aware of the blurred boundary between confused subjectivity and a genuine attempt to reflect critically. Reassured by Md. Anisur Rahman[2], that 'learning is a creative process that cannot be accomplished by a mechanical transfer of external knowledge', I realise that both critical reflection and creative application are vital to people's right to think for themselves. There is no single, simple truth in development –

and learning is after all grounded in personal experience and individual awareness.

Development practice is often an elaborate journey, taken with other travellers, during which, as best you can, you seek to nurture a sense of questioning. The learning, woven into the action, reflection, experience, and awareness, is central to the process of change and enriches it at every turn. If there has not been a shift in people's understanding of themselves and their own lives (and yourself and your life), then the development has failed.

As practitioners, we navigate our way as best we can with sensitivity – refining and reviewing to suit each community and situation. In working with people's intrinsic humanity, we need to use as much care, kindness and skill as a midwife at a birth. It is a craft, rich in meaning, learning, and connection – and change, uncertainty, and surprise.

> 'We need to develop the faculty of self-reflection, of humility in the face of unpredictability and uncertainty of life. We must recognise that we are most often in the dark when we are most certain and the most enlightened when we are most confused.'[3]

The Stages In The Mashabela Practice — March-October 1997

I have identified seven stages to the intervention, which although described as distinct, were not always clear cut. I have threaded some models and theories into the discussion and at the beginning of each section, I headline some of the roles that were picked up by local people or myself. The key events in each phase are summarised at the start of each section.

▌ Beginnings (7th March-7th April)

The Villagers	The Practitioner
Cautious Experimenters	*Brought in Outsider*
Engaged Participants	*Apprehensive Foreigner*
Valued Responders	*Confident Workshop Facilitator*

This phase started when Nong Makola first introduced me to the village on 7th March and it finished at the end of the first workshop, when there was an understanding that I would continue to work with them.

Local Choice

At the very first meeting, I was aware of the potential of the people, the time, and the place. The Mashabela Development Council had only just been formed, and on paper anyway, it seemed impressive . The people I met seemed to be open and committed to development, which confirmed my interest in working with them.

I wanted to be seen as a resource rather than as an expert. I offered to facilitate a workshop so they could see how I worked, and then decide if they wanted me to continue with them. Later I realised that it was naïve to expect them to be able to make such an explicit choice. They had little idea of what might be involved, and most had little or no experience of working with white people.

They obligingly went along with the notion that they had decided that I would continue to work with them, but in reality nothing tangible had been agreed that could be reviewed later. My role with the village was formally 'validated' by the village Council Executive a few weeks later, but there were no terms attached that would have enabled local people to question my work, or for me to check back with them as to how they felt we were doing. My lack of experience and confidence mirrored local peoples', and resulted in an *ad hoc* arrangement between us.

I learnt that people needed much more than a simple invitation to decide. They require information about options, and a sense of personal confidence in both the right to make the choice and some practice in actually doing it. Saying yes is almost always easier than saying no.

On reflection, however, there *was* benefit for Mashabela people to be invited to make a choice about my involvement with them. Some important principles that were new to the villagers were being embodied.

- Local people have an undeniable right to participate in making decisions in relation to their community and their lives.

- Development practitioners are resources to local communities. Their role is to enable local people to learn, work together, generate ideas, and take action. They should not behave as experts, who come in to impose external solutions.

The ground was being prepared for the way that we would work together. Although in hindsight, I would do some things differently, the benefit of actively applying personal values and principles was confirmed, whatever the development stage of the process or the outcomes on the day.

Why Was the Workshop Such a Success?

The planning process for the first workshop was poor because the women in the group had difficulty contributing. It was unrealistic to involve them in planning something that was so unfamiliar. However, as above, there was value in involving them. New behaviour has to be practised many times before it can be comfortably integrated.

The workshop itself was an undoubted success. Over thirty people attended, and many participated with real enthusiasm and obvious enjoyment. Many of the women found to their surprise that they could contribute their ideas in the small groups. The men were open to working in this new way with the women. All the workshop goals and more were realised and it was an extraordinary occasion – all the more for being the first development workshop ever run in the village.

Why was it such a success? What were the ingredients that allowed people to participate so fully?

In reflecting on what we did, there were a number of factors that were important, and which we replicated at subsequent workshops.

- Seating was arranged around tables in small discrete groups of five or six.

- Visibility was good – each table was on its own but people could see everyone else in the room.

- The workshop process was highly experiential (each exercise drew on familiar experience or asked for ideas about things that the participants knew about). It incorporated vision, which was positive, and generated a sense of optimism. It used experience (through the five senses) to ground the vision in reality.

- This was the first workshop of its type and therefore had novelty value. It was enjoyable and something of an occasion.

- Effective networking by Nong and others resulted in recruiting and preparing people active in village development – or those with good potential to be involved.

- The interpreter was well known, respected and liked in the village. He was an extrovert, which added to the sense of occasion. The facilitator was white and from England, which also contributed interest and intrigue.

- An agreement to have more than 50% women emphasised the value of the women's participation.

- A planning group had met to formulate goals. These were circulated before the workshop began.

- There was a clear structure within the workshop process (goals, programme, explanation of exercises and purpose, links made back to goals, etc.).

- The workshop was facilitated with respect for each contribution (all were written up on flipchart), interest in what was said, and awareness of what was happening.

In order to explore these 'enabling' conditions, I developed a simple model that I call the African House Model (see page 00). I use the metaphor of parts of a house to describe the conditions needed for a group to engage in learning about itself and be able to apply the learning by taking action together.

1. Safety and Structure within the Group Process

In the workshop this was achieved by arranging the seating to ensure good visibility, the goals, workshop structure, and the networking. By doing this, trust was developed and learning was able to flow.

2. Building Trust and Connection in the Group

The experiential process and the small group focus contributed to building trust and connection, especially within the groups, although this probably would not have survived the workshop.

3. Values underpinning the Process

The 50+% women quota, the planning process, and the style and approach of the facilitation, served to ground and embody the underpinning values.

4. Vision

The use of vision was important in supporting a positive focus, and generating a rare and enjoyable sense of optimism and positive possibility.

People need to feel safe, to understand what is going on, and to trust both those around them and the process itself, in order to **be open** to learn, to be aware, and to participate and connect. It is the openness that unfolds the rest.

A Quota for the Women

At the first meeting, I asked whether there could always be more women than men in every village group I worked with in Mashabela. I knew that usually the men would dominate numerically and in every other way. At the workshop, I was happily surprised by the contribution of the women. I assumed that the 50+% condition had given out a strong message that the involvement of the women was very important.

It was very different from what was happening inside the village, where women were commonly subordinate to men in every way. I knew it was vital to prioritise the participation of the women, but I was probably not fully aware of just how big a shift it implied.

In every society, community, organisation, and group there will always be a resistance to change and a desire to maintain the *status quo*. Initially, there did not appear to be any expression of this resistance in relation to prioritising the women. But a reaction of some sort was always likely, especially since the tradition of male supremacy is so strong. In the event, it came later during Women's Conference developments.

Through this, I learnt how important it is to acknowledge (or even seek out) the resistance to change and to work creatively with it. If the resistance is expressed, it can be incorporated as part of the process of change. It is tempting to let sleeping dogs lie, but they always wake up sooner or later.

In Mashabela, during and after this time, the women made some significant changes, but only some of them were sustained at a village level (rather than an individual one). More awareness of the resistance to change on my part may have made a difference and improved the chances of more sustained change.

Developing Shared Understanding

The workshop gave me a chance to ask myself some questions to help me gain clarity on possible directions and limitations.

- Were the conditions right for local Mashabela people to engage with broad community development processes?
- Would they become comfortable with me and the way I worked?
- Could we build enough trust together so that we could learn from each other?
- Would they be willing to explore my research with me? How might this work?

At this stage, I was unclear about how I would research the village development. In fact, it was only when I made the conceptual leap of seeing the whole – with the research within the action – that the research came to life. Later, it became obvious that the research interviews that I conducted in May and September were valued by the villagers, and that they added to the way that we started to articulate our understanding of what we were doing together and with each other.

There is much value in seeking out opportunities to be with people and reflecting with them on the process itself – and this is an important ingredient in action research. This way of being together is qualitatively different from the business of doing and planning and being busy. It is quieter somehow – more open and reflective. For the practitioner/questioner to listen and really hear the perspectives, feelings, and ideas of another can add new colour, texture, and shape to her own picture – that she would never see on her own. For the responder/local person to articulate ideas and feelings about her own experience and be really heard – can be immeasurably rich, empowering and affirming. Together, it is a mutual process that uncovers and shares meanings – forms connection and removes barriers – adds new learning – and has the potential to enrich the whole intervention.

2 Community Seen (7th April-30th April)

The Villagers

Willing Informers
Observed Observers

The Practitioner

Naïve Enquirer
Observing Observed

This relates to the period immediately after the first workshop, up to the formation of the Learning Group. During this time, I gathered information and learned about village organisation, structure, people, culture, history, problems, issues, and resources. I started to spend regular time in the village and in meetings with Nong Makola.

Grounded in Experience

As a complete outsider, with only a few months experience of the area, I was both excited and challenged by the prospect of working in Mashabela. There was so much to learn about the village and the issues affecting village people.

Initially, when I first arrived in Apel, I only had Northern cultural 'labels' to interpret what I was experiencing. I was more physically aware than usual, triggered by all the different sights, sounds, and smells around me. At first everything appeared very strange. At some point, when 'home' in the North moved further away in my mind and 'here' in the South became a little more familiar, the labels started to shift. I noticed more clearly how I was responding to experience and how I used to respond. The two situations (old and new) were somehow visible to me in a new way – and I experienced this on many levels, in my thinking and my emotions, and also in my physical sensory experience.

At the same time, there was a strong pull to belong and not be a stranger anymore – to establish roles and identity that would prop up my shaky sense of security. But conversely, it also felt liberating to be free of past baggage and just focus on life, as it was, with all the new experiences that were involved.

I found a special learning opportunity, in being in a different environment and culture to my 'usual' one. This can even happen, I believe, when the different situation is quite ordinary (for example when we move house or change jobs). While you are still in that groundless in-between place of belonging neither to the old nor the new, there is opportunity to learn things about ourselves our lives – both in the former environment or culture, and now in the context of the new. As soon as we respond to the pull to belong and appease that uncomfortable uprooted feeling within you, a new sense of self somehow gets reconfigured – and gradually we root ourselves into the new 'home' and lose that special awareness.

However, when the move is temporary and the differences in culture and environment are great, as was the case for me in South Africa, there are a number of repeated opportunities to experience this awareness. As development practitioners, it seems to me to be a precious opportunity, especially in terms of our own personal awareness and development – in helping us to develop insights and understanding about the people and situations we are working with – and in challenging and uncovering our assumptions, pre-conceptions and expectations.

Grounded in Experience[4]

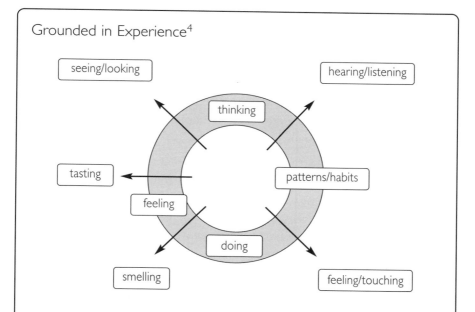

This model is a simplified representation of personal awareness.

The Inner Space represents the grounded, open, relaxed, and wise, loving and balanced aspect of self, which at an intrinsic level is pure awareness.

The Outer Ring represents the usual place that we live, caught up in the fog of automatic thinking, feeling and doing – often driven by habitual patterns and reactions – and without much clarity of awareness about our experience.

The Five Arrows represent the five senses, flowing from the inner space, through the outer ring into the 'world'. They are our the tools for awareness and the means to be more fully present – and to cut through the fog of our 'automatic pilot' and reduce the barriers to full awareness. The mind is sometimes considered as the sixth sense.

I learnt that living and working in a different culture and physical environment, greatly increased my sense of clear, immediate sensory awareness and offered me special opportunities to understand myself, my situation, and my values and responses.

Getting To Know and Getting Known

Every community is unique in its own way. It may look much the same as the neighbourhood next door, but there will be differences that speak clearly about the people, and their struggles and their lives. This was certainly so in Mashabela.

Although I was rapidly learning about them, Mashabela people probably always knew more about me. Being the only white person in the village (except the Catholic priest), I was always visible, and inevitably attracted attention. This was both an advantage, because it drew in the curious to get involved in meetings and development events, and a drawback, because it acted as a distraction from the focus of what was going on.

Once I had been there for a month or two, the pull to belong was strong and, at times, I simply forgot how different I was. Surrounded by familiar African faces, spending so little time with other white people, and immersed in the work of development – my sense of connection to the village and its people grew. It was not that I ever actually forgot that I was white, but as time passed, I was sometimes lulled into a strong, but ultimately unreal, sense of belonging.

I was surprised by the warmth of the friendships that I made with some of those that I worked most closely with. Other more casual village acquaintances were usually pleasant and friendly to me, but their attentions, especially in the early days, might easily move into a request for food, money or help with transport. This was not unexpected. But in my naïvety, I had assumed that there would be a measure of general distrust to overcome, between myself, as white, and the African villagers, who had long years of suffering under Apartheid. I never imagined that I would be welcomed in this way and I puzzled over this. Their friendships certainly seemed genuine – but in their place, if our situations were reversed, I doubted that I could get close to someone who I associated with such appalling oppression. Without wanting to idealise, I decided, after some time, that as people they were simply a lot more open, genuine and immediate than most of my own race, myself included. Being with them was a very wholesome experience and strangely inspiring.

When the German donors visited Mashabela towards the end of my time in the village, I was shocked and ashamed to be shown aspects of whiteness, which

I found quite out of tune with how I believed I was relating to the village. I was back again in the uncomfortable 'gap' between experiencing cultures, seeing things about myself and my own culture as if for the first time – questioning what I thought I knew and finding many ways to interpret my experience.

The villagers quickly returned to the familiar ways of relating to white people. The German visitors were treated as experts, who knew more than the villagers did about the village and their own condition. The Germans were shown respect as honoured guests, in the hope they would give the village money. The connection between white people and money was re-confirmed and the legacies of colonialism and dependency re-expressed. It was deeply depressing to witness.

I learned to appreciate that nothing is fixed, and old attitudes constantly reoccur. As uncomfortable as it is, it is crucial to be able to see things as they are, rather than as you would like them to be. How else can we work with what is real and what really matters? It is only our awareness that enables us to work with sensitivity. Without it we may perpetuate patterns that reconfirm injustice and dependency.

Learning About the Issues

In the early days, my role was to learn, listen, and build connections. I came to understand more about village issues – in terms of :

- levels of poverty and exclusion

- the condition of the women

- opportunities for young people

- disparities of access to development in the outer sub villages and

- overall health and infrastructure needs

You might say that little in that list is very different from disadvantaged areas anywhere – but my understanding of village needs became a dynamic process that involved one-to-one exchanges, rather than simply observing things at a distance and gathering data. Local people began to articulate their perspective, which added to their own understanding and allowed me to see a little of their world as they experienced it.

Gareth Morgan[5] believes that the process involves the beginning of building 'a holistic view of shared meanings'. Outsiders have an important role in the process of developing understanding, articulating local problems and finding local solutions. My learning confirmed the remarks made to me by Peter Derman in Durban some months earlier, that the researcher can act as a catalyst to local people in helping them to reflect on their stories and their essential condition.

3 Forming the Learning Group – Developing the Learning

The Learning Group	The Practitioner
Wide Eyed Recruit	*Connection Builder*
Early Learners	*Experimenting Learning Engineer*
Apprentice Practitioners	*Method Coach*
Light see-ers	*Mutual Learner/Facilitator*
Family Members	

As the Learning Group came together, I worked to build trust and connection in the group, which was important in enabling the women to participate alongside the men. This task of building and sustaining connection in the group was an ongoing one.

While this was happening, the Learning Group turned their attention to the development process and principles. They learned from their own experience of facilitating village development and from specific topics in the Learning Group. My role was as facilitator of this learning process.

The Idea for a Learning Group

As Nong Makola and I started meeting regularly, we looked at what might follow the first workshop. We decided to bring together a small group, which would have a focus on development learning. Elizabeth Metwane, one of the Learning Group members, in an interview with me, described the role of the group as learning 'how to develop (the village) and how to work together and take it to the people'.

Keeping the 50+% women composition, Nong and I chose people who had made significant contributions in the workshop, from different backgrounds and sub villages. Despite our efforts, we inevitably finished up with a lot of teachers, since they were already the most involved and confident.

The membership of the group was later adjusted by the members themselves, but I probably underestimated the significance of the group, and the status that would be conferred on it by the village. Wider representation, with fewer teachers, should have been possible, other selection methods may not have worked any better. In the end, there were five women and four men. They came from a range of different sub villages. The age range was limited, with few younger people, but the group did represent a fair amount of 'new blood' in terms of village development.

It took time to develop trust in the group, and it was easy to be over ambitious about what was possible. I was slow in appreciating what a huge adjustment was required for the men and women to work together.

The shifts, when they happened, were quite jerky. Occasionally, when there was no pressure, the group would soften and relate with gentleness and ease. When this happened, I sensed an engagement and resonance that was warm, open and enlivening.

As with the first workshop, I learnt that the enabling conditions were important to help the group work and learn together.

African House Model[6]

1. Fence and foundations		1. Safety and structure
2. House walls		2. Building trust and connnection
3. Garden		3. Underpinning values
4. Windows		4. Grounded vision
5. Roof		5. Overview
6. Door and the inside of the house		6. Learning and action

Using the African House Model ingredients:

1. Safety and structure: through familiar group rituals, boundary keeping, clarity of purpose, consistency, linking back to previous decisions/topics/sessions.

2. Trust and connection: through trust building processes, small group and pair discussions, modelling openness, warmth, and respect.

3. Underpinning Values: through making them explicit whenever possible, being aware of and agreeing about values, helping group (when ready) to determine and develop own values.

4. Grounded Vision: through a focus on what is positive and possible, grounded and balanced in experience (through five sense work), so that

vision is used to enhance creativity and free up what is possible whilst 'the feet' stay on the ground.

5. Overview: through relating back to the 'big picture' in the village and beyond.

6. Learning and Action: through the integration and practice of new behaviour and new learning – 'walking in the shoes of others' to gain understanding of their experience; taking small actions to concretise and integrate the learning. (see Experiential Learning Cycle below)

Starting To Learn Together

Meetings often started late and the attendance of the group was patchy. The women were often tied up with domestic and family commitments and some of the men lived some distance away. Although in principle we met weekly over five months, in reality it was hard to predict who would be present and how long we would actually have together. Sometimes the group felt very flat and tired. At other times they were bright and interested. I tried to work with this, but I also tried to keep going with my planned programme. This style, of course, was exactly what I wanted to avoid – that of teacher and students, with the implicit connotations of experts and dependency – but it was a style we were all familiar with and it also expressed the resistance to change within the system.

At first, I thought my role was to share my development knowledge. Later, on reflection, I realised that it was through the process of finding ways to 'translate' my development practice to them that my own learning blossomed. Through this process, I began to understand things differently, even within areas that were extremely familiar to me. In essence I was learning more about how I learnt, which helped me to facilitate a process that supported others to learn how to learn. The process was essentially mutual, and far from *me* 'giving' *them* knowledge, I was learning as much or more than they were. There is truth in the old adage – that the one who 'teaches' often learns the most. I learnt that the mutuality of this process is not just an advantage but an essential ingredient in congruent development learning – or learning to learn.

I learned that trusting the process is a powerful and courageous way to work. It needs you, as group worker and practitioner, to be fully present with what is going on – both in the group and within yourself. It requires a willingness to be open, to let go of trying to achieve the task, and to relax into the natural resonance of the group. Then the learning happens in an organic way that belongs to no-one and everyone.

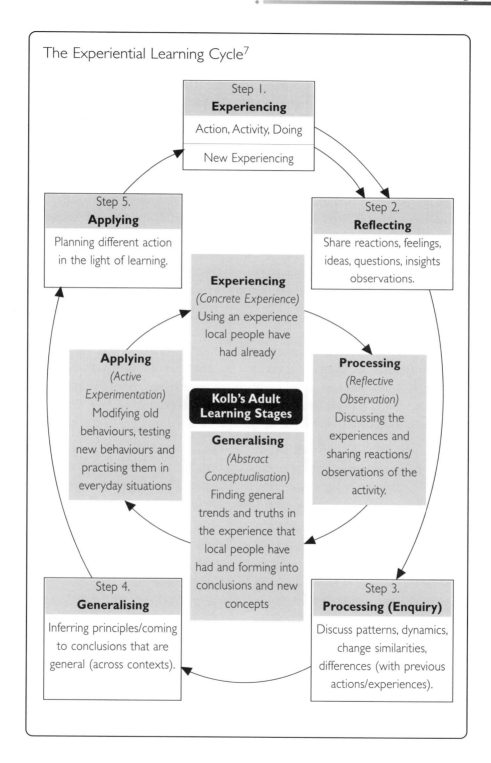

The Experiential Learning Cycle[7]

Step 1.
Experiencing

Action, Activity, Doing

New Experiencing

Step 5.
Applying

Planning different action in the light of learning.

Step 2.
Reflecting

Share reactions, feelings, ideas, questions, insights observations.

Experiencing
(Concrete Experience)
Using an experience local people have had already

Applying
(Active Experimentation)
Modifying old behaviours, testing new behaviours and practising them in everyday situations

Kolb's Adult Learning Stages

Processing
(Reflective Observation)
Discussing the experiences and sharing reactions/ observations of the activity.

Generalising
(Abstract Conceptualisation)
Finding general trends and truths in the experience that local people have had and forming into conclusions and new concepts

Step 4.
Generalising

Inferring principles/coming to conclusions that are general (across contexts).

Step 3.
Processing (Enquiry)

Discuss patterns, dynamics, change similarities, differences (with previous actions/experiences).

Learning Through Experience

David Kolb's Experiential Learning Cycle was familiar to me. I regret that I did not share it with the group explicitly. I believe it would have been helpful and interesting in clarifying and understanding the patterns that emerged.

I think I sometimes mistook uncertainty in the Learning Group for passivity or tiredness. When introducing a new subject (step 1), they would often seem flat. I would ask them how they were getting on, and they would reassure me that they were fine – but I felt that they were not. Later, when we went over similar material again, perhaps expressed in a different way or linked to something that they had recently experienced, they began to make a few tentative links and started to reflect (step 2). When they reviewed it (steps 2, 3 and 4), they were observing, feeling, and learning the significance for future action – and in the light of that, they made decisions as to the way they would act in the future (step 5). The penny began to drop and the learning was starting to be integrated into new behaviour.

I learned about the subtlety of the process. Even though I was familiar with models of experiential learning, all too often I would take personal responsibility for how the group reacted by assuming that their flat response was the result of my poor facilitation. It may have been, but they needed to 'go around' new learning several times and reflect on their own experience, before being able to understand it and apply it meaningfully. Their blank expressions were less likely to represent boredom than pensiveness and reflection.

Elizabeth Metwane referred to this when they were reviewing the second workshop. They were beginning to connect their Learning Group sessions with what was happening in the village process. She said 'There is light for us now. We understand more now that we learn more. This light lets us see where we are going'.

As village development started to get off the ground, the Learning Group members related to each other in a number of settings, which involved both planning and action. These experiences were brought back into the group through the commitment to review all development events that the Learning Group had a hand in running. They got into the swing of doing this and learned a lot from sharing and evaluating their experiences. It was during these reviews that their learning often really came together.

Developing new roles in this way is a bit like the struggle of a new born foal to find her feet. At first, it may take her time even to even stand up, and longer still to walk, until finally the foal can run with grace. In the same way, we too have to practise and practise in order to behave in a new way. At first, it always

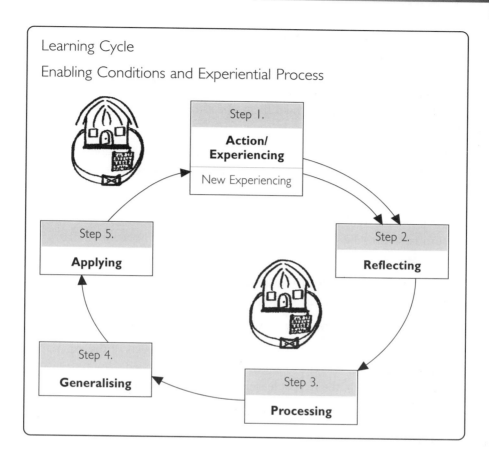

Learning Cycle

Enabling Conditions and Experiential Process

Step 1.

Action/ Experiencing

New Experiencing

Step 5.

Applying

Step 2.

Reflecting

Step 4.

Generalising

Step 3.

Processing

feels uncomfortable, as if we are pretending. As time passes and our practice develops, we stagger, walk, and then run – and finally the new behaviour comes naturally. It is only then that it is fully integrated in the full repertoire of our behaviour.

As my own learning went 'around', I realised that it might be useful to combine both models. The African House comes first – representing the enabling conditions that are necessary to allow the group to get to a point (step 1) where they can learn from the experience/action they have taken. In the review (steps 2, 3 and 4), the group also needs the enabling conditions (African House) to feel confident about being able to reflect, process and infer conclusions, and then move on to apply this learning to plan different actions (step 5) in the light of the review.

The Experiential Learning Cycle is a useful model that is widely used and respected, but while it describes the process of learning, it leaves open the question of how people get to a place where they are able to learn. In essence it describes an intellectual process to learning, which omits some vital ingredients and dimensions that are linked to experience and emotion. The African House model offers an understanding of the conditions that are needed to enable the participants to participate. Without them, the learning may not ever start to take place.

In the Learning Group we used the old faithful, review questions (which, of course, is a direct but simpler version of Kolb's Experiential Learning Cycle).

We asked:

1. What worked well? (Went according to plan? Better than we hoped? Pleasant surprises? How did you feel? How did it compare with previous similar experience? etc.)

2. What did not work well? (Disappointing? Problem? Difficult? Surprising? How did you feel? How did it compare? etc.)

3. What would we do differently (if we were doing it again now)? Why?

This simple process basically explores the positive aspects of the experience, the negative aspects, and the changes that could be applied, based on lessons learned. As with Kolb, the richest learning takes place when people:

- feel safe and secure enough to participate

- experience trust and connection with their fellow learners

- are encouraged and enabled to 'go around' each new learning to experience it in different ways several times

4 From Vision To Planning To Training (1 July-5 August)

The Learning Group

Budding Leaders
Interpreting Facilitators
Responsible new role planners and players

The Practitoner

Guardian of the Boundaries
Sessional Skills Trainer
Odd Jobbing Car Driver

The Villagers

Enthusiastic Junior Facilitators
Competent Census Takers
Reflexive Perspective Shifters

Backseat Adviser
Two Fingered Typist
Certificate designer

This phase moves the Learning Group out into the village. It starts with the second workshop, where it was decided to hold a large village meeting to share the plans and consult with older village members, and includes all the planning and training that followed:

- *Facilitator Team Training*
- *Census Team Training*
- *Women's Conference Planning*
- *Leadership Workshop.*

My role, from this point on, was focussed on skills training. I was withdrawing from influencing the way ideas were formed, and moving into the role of adviser and encourager.

The Significance of the Second Workshop

The second workshop, delayed by the death of the Chief, was held to involve others in sharing and shaping the village plans. The decision that came out of it, to hold a large village meeting to involve the older men, was very significant. Without their approval and understanding, things might have foundered. It was a creative and important decision, which I did not at first appreciate. The Learning Group understood the significance and pointed it out to me. This was an important highlight, and a watershed in the whole intervention.

Focal Conflict Model

Looking at this in the light of the Focal Conflict model[8] developed by Lieberman, Lakin and Whitaker, it is easy to see why the decision to involve the older men was so important.

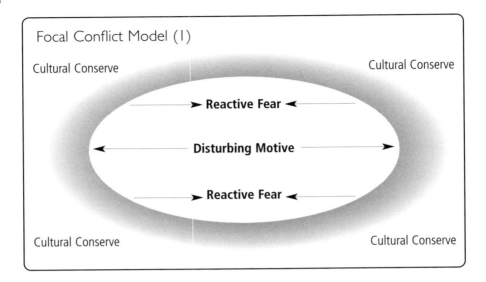

Looking at change and conflict in groups and organisations, the focal conflict model offers a useful picture of the change process, like a ripple in a pond going out and coming back, constantly moving in both directions until the energy of the ripple is spent.

The ripple is first initiated when an idea is proposed that presents a new development. This is known as the Disturbing Motive. It reacts with the Cultural Conserve (at the edges of the pond), which represents members of the group or community that want to maintain the *status quo* and keep traditional norms, and are fearful of change and/or being different. This energy is called the Reactive Fear, which expresses the conserve and is always present whenever a new idea is proposed. It is not necessarily negative and may act as a protection against change ideas that are inappropriate or dangerous.

Out of this drama comes one of two possible solutions. The Enabling Solution expresses both directions of the 'ripple' – both the creative change involved in the Disturbing Motive and the Reactive Fear expressed in the cultural conserve. If an Enabling Solution cannot be found, the conflict (and opportunity for change) is shut down through the use of a Restrictive Solution, which alleviates the Reactive Fear, retains the status quo and prohibits expression of the Disturbing Motive. If both aspects can be expressed (the Disturbing Motive and the Reactive Fear), it is possible to integrate the change into the culture of the group and a move forward can be made. The group will be the healthier when able to identify and apply enabling solutions and allow new disturbing motives to come through.

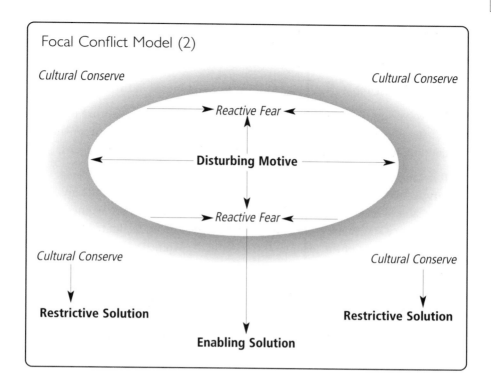

Focal Conflict Model (2)

In Mashabela, the disturbing motive was the proposal to encourage ordinary members of the village (women and young people) to participate in development activity. This was very different from how things were usually done. The reactive fear felt by the second workshop participants prompted them to recognise that the older men, who used to make all the decisions in the village, had not yet been involved or consulted. The cultural conserve in this instance was the respect shown to the wisdom and experience of the older men. By deciding to hold a Village Meeting, the workshop participants found an enabling solution that allowed expression of both the traditional and the new. They were highly successful in finding a way of moving forward, by bringing everyone along with them and inviting the expression of all views.

This decision was a pivotal point in the village process, and picked up its own momentum after this, facilitated by the Learning Group and members of the Executive. They took up the reins of village leadership and started to execute development plans. My job was to support and affirm them, and to facilitate their learning by reviewing the action with them.

The village meeting was run with skill, confidence, and efficiency by members of the Learning Group and Executive, who took turns to speak about different aspects of the proposed village process. This allowed them to own and understand the plans more fully – going round the experiential learning cycle – in a way that built their confidence and understanding of the process.

Later I realised that the Village Meeting was significant in three distinct ways.

1. It involved and incorporated the traditional 'authority' and culture in the village – the older men – who expressed interest and enthusiasm for the development plans and, in effect, conferred their blessing on the plans.

2. It involved significant numbers of 'new' developers. Young people came forward to volunteer to be trained in the Facilitators and Census Teams, and a sizeable group of women came forward to start planning the Women's Conference. These people, and others who joined them, facilitated the key village processes of the Maololo Process and the Women's Conference.

3. It allowed the emergent development leaders (The Learning Group and some of the Executive) to understand the plans in a fuller way, which facilitated an expanded sense of ownership and confidence.

It is interesting that the decision to hold the Village Meeting evolved out of the development process of itself, and out of the awareness of local people that the older men had not been involved. Seen now in the context of the Focal Conflict Model, it is apparent that the decision to consult the older men also opened the door to involving large numbers of women and young people in an empowering way. The Chief's funeral, falling as it did between the second workshop and the Village Meeting, was a perfect opportunity to promote the occasion.

It might not have been like that – but by preparing the ground as we did, the process was able to unfold in a way that had its own rightness and truth. Through an intention to share ideas with people who are usually left out; listen to those not often heard; respect customs that had existed for years; and incorporate different points of view wherever they came from, the process was allowed to evolve, like a river finding its course to the sea. This is a subtle thing – flexible but not entirely without form. We learnt that it was possible to bring together both the traditional and the newly created in a way that offered more to both.

'Until one is committed there is always hesitancy,
the chance to draw back, always ineffectiveness
concerning all acts of initiative and creation
there is one elementary truth
the ignorance of which kills countless ideas and splendid plans:

All sorts of things occur to help that would never otherwise have occurred.
A whole stream of events issues from the decision,
Raising to one favour all manner of unforeseen accidents and meetings
and material assistance which no man could have dreamed
    would come his way.
Whatever you can do or dream you can, begin it.
Boldness had genius, power and magic in it'

Goethe

The Women's Conference Planning

Over 100 women were involved at different times in the weekly meetings in the Tribal Office to plan the Women's Conference. These included many who had never before been involved in any village development activity. Their discussions in Northern Sotho were always bright and energetic, but since a different group gathered each week, it was hard to see how it would all come together. They chose their own leaders, including several from the Learning Group, and each leader was given a 'department' to run, such as food and cooking, fund raising, drumming and dancing groups, and so on.

I acted as 'guardian' of the boundaries, ensuring that the women had the room to themselves for their meetings. I was probably the only one who could get away with asking the men to leave the room.

The planning process contributed to the sense of growing involvement and enthusiasm in the women for the conference. Whilst the outcomes were hard to predict, their sense of engagement was evident. The meetings were full of laughter and noise, with several discussions happening at the same time. The process seemed chaotic, but only in relation to the planning of the conference. There were also many glimpses of very healthy patterns, such as the leadership roles, the participation, the enjoyment, the new behaviour (meeting without the men), and the connection between the women.

Sometimes out of confusion comes creativity. There is always risk, it seems. The conference could easily have fallen on its face and reconfirmed the women's dependence on the men for all events. But when there is energy of spirit, there is the chance that the natural rightness of the process will survive the confusion and incipient chaos – and allow a space for the spirit to dance.

As Md. Anisur Rahman writes about the Bhoomi Sena movement in Maharashtra, India:

'The emerging sense of participation is closely identified with spontaneity, which is the primary source of human creativity, and with self-reliance...The task is delicate – to develop spontaneity and self-reliance in such necessary interaction with their opposites (organisation and dependence) without being taken over by the latter may indeed be the central internal problem in efforts...to promote participation.'[9]

Facilitators and Census Team Training

Both the Facilitators and the Census Teams were predominantly composed of young people, who seemed enthusiastic. By this point, we had refined the workshops by applying the learning that had come out of the reviews. We now used an interpreter from the Learning Group, who was familiar with my way of working and had been part of deciding on the aims of the training. This moved the workshop process on and improved it a lot. The workshop programmes were more realistic, allowing the groups to dictate the pace. It was easier now to establish safety and trust within each training group.

The Census Team Training got off to a difficult start, when we found that it was oversubscribed by three times the number needed. Some people had to be turned away, which was quite out of tune with how we were trying to work. In hindsight we could have run several courses, in English and Sapedi, irrespective of the census team task – so that all young people who wanted, could have benefited from training in communication skills. Instead, we were focussed on our development programme and already pushed for time.

It is easy to spot the moment afterwards, when task becomes more important than process, and time becomes the main constraint. When the emphasis is on completing agreed programmes, responsiveness and flexibility go out the window, sometimes with the loss of precious opportunities. The treadmill has been created and it is all too easy to keep going round without question. I have learned the importance of review at every point, especially when new circumstances arise, so that it is always possible to change plans and do things differently.

In both workshops, experiential exercises were used to facilitate learning about communication, body language, and the conditions that enable people to be fully involved. As they learnt through their own participation, the villagers were able to 'go around' the learning cycle, practising new roles as they went.

This period was busy and rewarding. The Learning Group were rapidly developing their leadership roles and undertaking many new responsibilities. The issues discussed in our sessions were now being played out in a way that offered them real practice and opportunity for integration. Each part of the development process was contributing to building the capacity and developing the learning of groups and individuals – sometimes quite powerfully.

'African Time'

No-one turned up for the arranged second census team day training. Meetings often started late in Mashabela, but most usually got going eventually. It turned out that a local football match and a wedding party had kept the young people away. When we rearranged to meet a few days later, all but one of the original group returned. I chose not to express my frustration at the time I had wasted.

If there had been a contract with the village, with terms and understandings about my role and goals of our work, I might have felt more confident about challenging people when I was left waiting for meetings to start. Without it, issues like time were slithered over. When I returned to the village two years later, I refused to run a workshop when participants turned up over two hours late. If we had done that in 1997, several key meetings would never have happened.

There is value in facing difficult issues. It requires a level of awareness both about personal feelings and responses, and also, about the context for others. It may be easier to slide over a problem and pretend an issue does not exist, but sharing difficulties, without apportioning blame, can also be very productive. It opens things up and demonstrates congruence between values and action, showing a commitment to share responsibility and ownership. This is empowering action.

In Mashabela it was standard that almost every meeting and workshop started late. At one level, it was a way of giving me a strong message about their power to make choices. But if I had raised the issue, I might have enabled local people to be more aware, able to make different choices, and take responsibility for them.

5 Walking The Walk – Implementation (16 August-26 September)

The Learning Group

Implacable Warriors
Mistress of Ceremonies Extraordinaire
Leading Light Public Speakers
Competent Gap Fillers
Assured Village Leaders

The Practitioner

Guardian of the Boundaries
Three Fingered Typist
Nail Chewing Participant
Affirming Debriefer/Reviewer
Unhappy Chicken Transporter

The Villagers

Dancing Conference Go-ers
Enthusiastic Village Planners
Courageous Well Digging Deciders
Participatory Riding High Village Developers

This phase involved all the key events in the development intervention – led by the Learning Group including:

- *Maololo sub village meetings (in which the facilitators ran small group discussions and the census team collected hard data about the community) and over 50% of the entire sub village gathered under one tree to decide on their development priority – and decided later at a subsequent meeting to dig out and line their village well;*

- *Women's Conference (250+) run, organised, planned, and funded by women themselves with outside speakers.*

My role was a supportive one, attending and speaking at all the events and involved in many admin tasks, since I had access to a computer, printer, telephone, and car to transport things and could run errands. I facilitated reviews within the Learning Group, sometimes involving others from outside the group in an attempt to 'join up' developments and apply learning as to how they might do it differently another time.

Maololo's Water

The Maololo meeting was one of the high points of the whole period. A planning group within Maololo (involving women and young people) had prepared the ground well, and the majority of the village was present (except the very old and the men who worked away). People from other sub villages walked many miles to

Maololo to be part of the meeting. The afternoon almost had a sense of village carnival.

The process had been designed to involve Maololo villagers in an active way, in small group discussions. This worked well, with the young facilitators doing a good job of supporting the small groups, which were animated and full of energy – except in the men's area, where unsurprisingly the few men present chose to remain in one large group. The census team also fulfilled their role well, going round to every household the following week collecting information about the population, and then collating it and passing the data on to the Executive.

When a smaller meeting happened a month later, to hear the technical advice of the water engineer, the women made an unexpected decision to dig out the wells themselves. At one level, their decision was spontaneous, grounded in the experience of being involved in the large meeting, of being included and affirmed. But the confidence of their decision also demonstrates the capacity of people to act in ways that predominantly benefit others. The process of including Maololo reinforced a sense of community, and included people usually left out – which allowed those people, the Maololo women, to act in ways that reinforced and benefited their community. The resonance within the village resulted in tangible action that was remarkable for its courage and initiative.

The Maololo women reminded me of the writing of Md. Anisur Rahman, who first inspired my research, who taught me that the creative potential of the person is intrinsic to her primary human dignity.

Maololo, before the start of the sub village process, was probably one of the sub villages furthest away from the 'centre' (Moshate) of the village. This affected their experience of belonging and their involvement in decisions and village activities.

Once the sub village process got underway, Maololo started to change, both within itself and in relation to Mashabela. A Maololo villager told me that he felt 'brought in' to the rest of the village and as he said this, it was clearly an emotional experience for him, that related to his sense of belonging, connection – and even of core personal identity.

Through seeing the changes to Maololo, I learnt about the value of appreciating the whole system and how it inter-relates. Maololo was part of a bigger whole and as their relationship to Mashabela changed, a resonance between all parts of the village system seemed to occur – which reinforced connection and inclusion. It seemed to be apparent that if you work with one part of a system, facilitating changes that benefit its members – all other parts of the system will be affected and may benefit too.

Outcomes and Disappointments

After such potential, it was sad and disappointing therefore, when I returned in 2000, to hear that Maololo was still using polluted water from their old wells. Other events had occurred that looked very promising at the time, but had come to nothing – in fact they had set the village back. Agencies and workers who had promised help had left the area, and no funding or support had been found to dig out the wells. Funding is now said to be allocated by the TLC for a water system for Maololo, but as far as I know no work has yet started.

This, of course, happens all the time to isolated communities, which are repeatedly marginalised, even when their neighbours' conditions start improving. In fact this very process of the improvement of neighbouring communities may result in increasing the marginalisation of the isolated one. Funding can eventually be found for the majority – in the case of Mashabela, those sub-villages which are close to the main road and to Moshate (the centre). The remote communities, which lie over the river or on the other side of the mountains, have their infrastructure developed much later – if ever. In purely economic terms, of course, you can provide water, electricity, and telephones to far more people at less cost, if you target the central communities. You get so much less for your money when you provide facilities to villages which are further away like Maololo.

Exclusion and poverty are therefore reinforced over and over, even in rural areas, like Mashabela, which themselves have long been excluded. People who have waited a long time for water and other basic developments find themselves going along with decisions based on the interests of the majority. It is hard to imagine them denying their own chance of a new water system because they insist that all their communities receive it at the same time. And yet, one could argue that unless we all do that, the patterns of poverty and inequality will continue and communities like Maololo, and many like them, will remain excluded and marginalised. Others might argue that we can only work to do the greatest good for the greatest number with the resources that are available.

The work we did in the Learning Group on power and elites was too little, too late, and not well enough integrated to make enough impact to benefit Maololo and their water. I was quite wrong in assuming that the agencies that moved into Mashabela would continue to develop the involvement of the women, young people *and* sub-villages on the extremities.

Robert Chambers, in his seminal book *Rural Development – Putting the Last First*[10] writes about the exclusion of people at the margins and how we can work differently to make a difference. 'Small gains well consolidated as part of a sequence can mean more than big gains which are unstable and short lived. Small moves to put the last first, all count, and they add up. It is action that matters…but knowing does not guarantee a change of feeling; and a change of feeling does not guarantee a change of behaviour…It is often best to start, to do something, and to learn from doing'.

We did make a start, we did learn from what we did, and some small changes *were* achieved. The interests of the sub villages are now represented on the Development Council and in committees and networks throughout Mashabela. The sub village process that started with Maololo highlighted the importance of listening to 'outer' viewpoints. It is an example of a small but consolidated gain that Robert Chambers writes about, but it was not enough to get clean water into Maololo.

Talane – Action Not Words

Talane, the next sub village to take up the challenge of looking at their development needs, put action before anything else. They held their meeting without facilitators or small group discussions – and these would probably have been dominated by the men. How could it be otherwise? Unless steps are taken to actively facilitate a different process, the cultural norm will always pre-dominate. They picked up on the action component of the process, and in no time had collected money and dug and laid the foundations of a new building for their pre-school children. I was invited to see this and photograph their efforts, and, a bit to my dismay, found the women doing all the heavy labouring work, collecting the sand from the road and mixing the cement, whilst the men did the more skilled work of laying the bricks.

It was interesting to compare the two villages and ask who benefited most. Which was the more sustainable?

Talane eventually finished their pre-school and improved their community facilities entirely through their own efforts. Local people made decisions and took action in a way that was self-reliant, clear, and effective. However, unlike Maololo, the position of the women was reinforced rather than challenged, there was little change in patterns of participation, and I doubt that much personal learning resulted, except to confirm that the cultural conserve, the old ways, are best.

Maololo, on the other hand, involved over 50% of the entire village in a highly participatory process that emphasised the value of inclusion and prioritised the involvement of the women and the learning of the young people. The process expressed the values of participation and equality – and resulted in an extraordinary display of courage and commitment by the women. The Maololo example appears to contain learning, change potential (power), and build community inclusion. A more pragmatic approach might argue that the value of a solid building is worth more than the lack of tangible outcome in Maololo, but I would not.

Looking at this another way, and analysing Talane and Maololo development in task and process, one could argue that Talane had a high task/action component and low process – whilst Maololo had high process component and (in the event) low task/action (although their intention at the second meeting was to move straight into action). The ideal would be a community development that has both high process *and* high task/action components.

The Women's Conference

The learning from the Women's Conference was also rich, flowing out of a quite different style of process. The women found that many of their assumptions about their own abilities were challenged. By successfully running the conference themselves, they discovered that they could plan, fund, organise, and take part in an event, entirely without the men's presence or help. They surprised themselves by how well they managed. This in itself was a significant achievement, but in the context of the challenge from the men and the difficulties with the RWA and the garden women, it was an extraordinary accomplishment and one that rightly affirmed the women. This message was underlined by a member of the ANC Women's League at the conference, who passionately proclaimed the power and value of women's participation in village matters. Over two years later, the women were still talking about the conference with a strong sense of pride and enjoyment.

The open planning process was what lay behind the success on the day. Not only had the women together decided how it would run and what would happen, but they had also 'naturally' publicised the event throughout the whole village to their friendship, neighbourhood, and sub village networks. No posters were needed to advertise the date or venue, because every village woman already knew about it. Through participating in the planning process, they felt as if they owned a share of the event, and could therefore feel confident about attending and bringing friends, sisters, daughters, and neighbours with them. Once there, they had a good time, singing, dancing, and hearing about the power of women to make a difference. This was the first time that the women had heard this sort of 'consciousness-raising' message in a development context.

There were many risks inherent in the Women's Conference. All sorts of things could have gone wrong, including repercussions with the men after it was over – but in the event, there was far more benefit than harm. The actual impact of the conference on the women was hard to definitively judge, but by 2000, they were confidently leading and running their own events, and starting to move into leadership roles in school governing bodies.

The 'Edge' Between the Village and Village Development

The argument between Nong and I strongly challenged us both and was probably one of the most dramatic threads of the intervention – involving a showdown and (happily) a resolution.

It also brought into stark focus, a challenging edge to my development practice.

At my first meeting in the village and consistently thereafter, I had insisted on working with 50% women in all the groups I was involved with. There was no agonising over this as an issue for me. I introduced it pretty much as a pre-condition to my involvement. The participation of the women was clearly crucial. Anything else would be colluding with the dominance of the men, reinforcing the *status quo* and supporting an oppressive system. Anything else would not have been community development as I sought to practice it.

However, it was also important to me, to overtly and deliberately show respect for the existing cultural conventions of the village, which sometimes involved going along with practices that I was not so keen on. There were many times at the Chief's funeral and in other village events, when the women were put down (with me amongst them). But I deliberately chose to tread a careful line that differentiated between development processes and village events. In development processes that I had a hand in facilitating, (or supported others to facilitate), I believed it was important to review the ways we were working, in the light of development principles. Working to increase the participation of women was a consistent goal of the Learning Group.

When interests diverged, things were less clear and different sets of cultural values and practice rubbed up against each other.

The Women's Conference had always been an important development process, owned by the women, with the overt aim of increasing the participation of the women in their own development, and in the wider development of the village as a whole. However, the week before it was due to take place, it also became a significant village event, once outside speakers were involved and threats and allegations were made from outside. These factors turned the tables, and transformed the Women's Conference into first and foremost a village occasion which, in the eyes of the men, required their involvement. In conditions like these, the men always had the role of protecting the village from threat and representing village authority.

Of course, I did not see this so clearly at the time. I struggled with my part in it. I questioned the wisdom of what I had done and whether there were things I should do differently. At each new development in the drama, I tried to check out my practice with my principles. On the one hand I had a responsibility to facilitate and support development in a way that promoted just, equitable and empowering opportunity for the women and on the whole, I felt I had been true to this. On the other hand, I had a strong ethical commitment not to waltz in, as a 'values colonialist', insisting on ways of working that were not appropriate to the culture I was working in.

In this situation, it seemed impossible to do both. I learned how powerfully difficult it is to stay engaged and grapple with conflicts that involve values and practice.

In working with situations like these, I saw the temptation of getting drawn into positions of guilt and blame. In the North, we seem to move readily into seeing issues of diversity in stereotypes and defining terms within hierarchies of oppression, where there are victims, and perpetrators, and sometimes rescuers. It is hard then to be true to ourselves – stereotypes become safer to hold on to – than our own personal learning.

In Mashabela, I had no clear answers and could only reflect on the uncomfortable edges in an attempt to balance challenge with respect; development with culture; empowerment with integration – and hope that whatever paths we had taken in the final analysis, no-one would be harmed.

As a woman, I felt challenged by Nong's position – but there was much about him that I respected – including his passionate conviction. Thanks to the outcomes of the conference (the men did *not* intervene and the women *did* run the event successfully), our row evaporated quickly. Later we were able to reflect on this together.

As it turned out, the conference could be said to have made a small start in developing different working relationships between the men and the women; by supporting the participation, leadership, and capacity of the women in a way that, in the end, was accepted by the men. Certainly, both the men and the women were surprised at the scale and success of the event.

In summary, the learning from the conference:

- affirmed the capacity of women to do things for the very first time
- reinforced the value of taking risks
- showed the wisdom of sticking to principles and hoping for the best
- demonstrated the effectiveness of an open planning process in sharing ownership, building confidence, and reaching into networks
- affirmed the power of participation and the value of having fun

Coming to the End of One Period and the Start of the Next

On 13th August, the Learning Group embarked on a review of their own activity – having already reviewed all the different initiatives. They affirmed significant learning, especially in the area of personal confidence and leadership. Some of them also expressed regret that they had not done more with young people. They expressed their belief in the importance of empowering young people, of training them to walk in the shoes of their elders, and decided to invite more young people into the Learning Group.

6 As One Leaves, Others Arrive

The Villagers   The Practitioner

Reactive Optimists   *Over-heated Party Guest*
Reviewing Reflective Departer
Unsure Outsider On Way Out

Exhausted Meetings Attenders

This phase marks the end of my role as practitioner – and as I was leaving, others were flocking into the village to run projects and training courses in this now 'active' village.

On the face of it the response and interest, shown in the village, by outside agencies was very encouraging. Some of them appeared out of the blue, presumably having heard about all the new development activity. Others responded to direct requests from members of the Executive and Learning Group for help in specific areas (water, legal constitution, financial management etc.). In the three weeks before I left, there were eleven separate meetings in the village, initiated by four NGOs and two government departments. All of a sudden, Mashabela was on the map and linked into regional development networks and initiatives. How could the villagers not be pleased? Just six months before, only the Catholic Church, a very small Department of Health Clinic and the RWA (the women's gardens) had any presence in the village.

I was too busy with reviews, farewells, and trying to get last tasks finished, to reflect much on what was coming next. It was as if there was a line drawn in the sand that denoted the end of one period and the start of another. Things felt very different to me with the advent of so many new practitioners and projects. As the one on the way out, I did not feel I had much of a role – and it simply did not feel much like my business any more. I was no longer **the** village development practitioner, just one of many.

Whilst this new situation, of being offered projects and training, must have seemed, at first, like a dream come true to the villagers, it soon developed into a bit of a nightmare, making impossible demands on their time and energy. Understood in the light of the Focal Conflict Model.

1. As the avalanche of change (disturbing motives) made itself felt, through all the many demands of meetings and training

2. The cultural conserve was strongly expressed

3. Through reactive fear, that change was threatening the fabric of power and connection in the village, and

4. A restrictive solution was found, which dealt with the threat of the change by reverting to old patterns of village participation, with the men making the decisions

I should also add that since I was not there for much of the time, except at the very beginning, this picture is based on my theorising, and conjecture, and a few conversations with local people on my return in 2000.

It would have been difficult to come up with an enabling solution. They would have had to find a way to integrate both the forces that feared the change, and the change itself. Even an established organisation, facing this level of upheaval, might have struggled. Some members of the village had learnt a lot through the activity of the previous six months, but six months is not long enough to fully integrate new learning and stay grounded in the experience.

The outcome was predictable and as local activity and participation waned, so for one reason or another, the projects and workers pulled out. As far as I know the sanitation project was the only one to be completed.

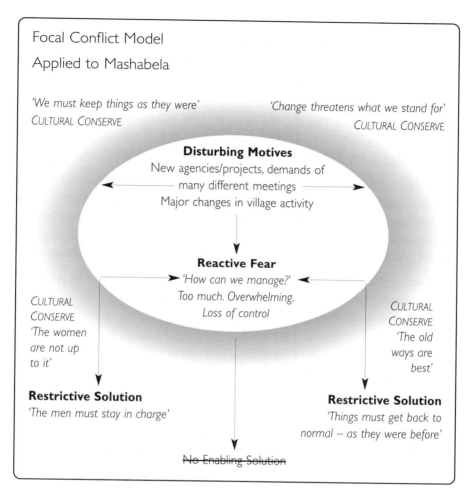

Focal Conflict Model

Applied to Mashabela

'We must keep things as they were'
CULTURAL CONSERVE

'Change threatens what we stand for'
CULTURAL CONSERVE

Disturbing Motives
New agencies/projects, demands of
many different meetings
Major changes in village activity

Reactive Fear
'How can we manage?'
Too much. Overwhelming.
Loss of control

CULTURAL
CONSERVE
'The women
are not up
to it'

CULTURAL
CONSERVE
'The old
ways are
best'

Restrictive Solution
'The men must stay in charge'

Restrictive Solution
'Things must get back to
normal – as they were before'

~~No Enabling Solution~~

How Could It Have Been Different?

In hindsight, I would have shaped my last few months rather differently. Rather than running the Leadership Workshop with a focus on individual learning, which had limited benefit, I would have suggested working with the Executive and Learning Group combined, to prepare and plan for what came next. We could have learnt about leadership in the context of the village. Together they might have been able to see the big picture, and anticipated the opportunities and threats that lay inside and outside the village.

I could have facilitated various techniques to help the villagers see things from a wider perspective. We could have drawn pictures on the floor, used objects and/or people to represent aspects of the village, outside agencies, departments, and funding bodies. We could have used Sociodrama and role-played the practitioners coming into the village, in order to gain some insights into what they might want. Techniques like these would have helped the villagers to understand things better, and develop ways of working that might have improved their chances of consolidating the changes and achieving enduring developments.

I should also have given more thought to ways of supporting Alta, Annah, Elizabeth, Molefe, and Therdla, the women in the Learning Group. This might have helped them be more confident and perhaps better able to continue working with the men in the Executive, once I had left.

However, hindsight is a wonderful thing and sadly, I regret that I did none of that. The initial failure to establish a clear contract with the village affected the process right up to the end. It was never possible to conduct a proper review of what we had done together, except within the Learning Group, which was valuable, but limited, since it did not reach the central decision-making village structure.

However there is also an important role for the practitioner to let go of the process, and trust that learning comes out of many situations, including challenge and difficulty.

Evaluation of Outcomes that Endured – Village Developments

By early in 1998 most of the NGOs and government agency staff had left the village, and things were returning to 'normal'. The only project left was the sanitation project, which created some temporary local jobs, ran some training, and built a number of new VIPs (Ventilated Improved Pit Latrines).

As the agency workers left and the projects faded, the village returned to how it had been, with the men in the Executive and the elders in the Tribal Council at the centre of village decision making. The ripples in the pond died out.

So from this position:

- What had endured from the development intervention of the year before?
- Were there any outcomes of our work that lasted?

Based on conversations and interviews with local people, it seemed that even though the village 'pond' looked as if it had returned to how it had always been, there were some changes, which, although subtle, seemed to have been consolidated.

The Learning Group never met again. As I understand it, there was an intention to continue, but things got so busy and the focus moved away, so by the time things calmed down, the moment had passed. But members of the Learning Group were active in village committees and initiatives, and some of them, especially the women, reported that they felt they had changed and were more confident in meetings and in their role as leaders. They were accorded a certain status within the village for having been members of the Learning Group, and this may have given them some additional influence.

The sub village process also failed to develop any further. All available energy was needed for the agency projects. However, influenced by Maololo and the aims of the sub village process, the Executive decided to include a representative from each sub village in all meetings and in the composition of village committees. This development, which still endures, is potentially including the outlying communities in an important way.

There was a feeling that the women were more active generally, and had stronger leaders who were doing a good job with the women's projects. They appeared less dependent on the Mission and the RWA. The young people similarly were felt to be participating with more confidence, although the generation of young people involved in 1997 had left for work or college in the cities by 2000.

The Executive successfully negotiated the formal instalment of the young Queen as the new Chief of Mashabela in 1999, both within the village and with the statutory authorities. This was a significant achievement, since it was still unusual to have a woman in the position of Kgosi. The Executive also managed to forge a better connection with the local TLC (Transitional Local Council) and in due course were able to have their own village representative at Council meetings. Interestingly, they chose a young woman to represent Mashabela. The Executive also successfully established an ANC branch in the village. Soon after this, Mashabela received funding for a water system for most of the village. This might have happened anyway, but it was a good decision to work to improve relationships with the funding body that supported village development.

At the end of 1997, Mashabela Council became a member of Tlhavhama, a regional umbrella training NGO. For at least three years, people from the village regularly attended training events in the then Northern Province (now known as Limpopo). This development linked Mashabela to other villages, CBOs and NGOs in the region, kept them informed about issues such as HIV/AIDS, and offered them high quality training and development support.

A village Agriculture Project got off the ground in 1998, initiated by Nong Makola with village women, many from Moshate. Land previously cultivated in family plots was jointly ploughed and irrigated. This has resulted in increased yields and improved quality of crops, and has enabled the women to come together and participate in training. Nong Makola attended college in Polokwane and after three years was successfully awarded a Diploma in Management and Development Studies.

Of course there are many influences on development and these outcomes will be the result of a number of factors.

7 Returning To Evaluate (20th March-9th May 2000)

The Villagers	The Researcher/former Practitioner
Willing Warm Interviewees	*Returning Friend*
Politicking New Guard	*Reflective Outsider again*

This final stage involves my return to Mashabela nearly 2 1/2 years after I left, to evaluate the outcomes of the 1997 process. I was there for seven weeks to interview people from the Learning Group and the Executive. I worked closely with Nong Makola and Molefe Sello, both former Learning Group members, who contributed information and ideas and facilitated the evaluation process. I tried but failed to meet with the village Executive to involve them in the evaluation. Village politics were in flux and the young Queen was elevating her own circle of young people into positions of power and moving the old guard out.

Those I interviewed described rich layers of personal learning that they linked directly to what we had done together. Some of them said (to differing degrees) that they had changed and had a deeper sense of connection to their fellow villagers. Some commented that, through working with me, they had changed their attitude to white people. They could see more similarities, and felt less wary and more able to stand alongside them. They said they were aware of their expertise in relation to local knowledge, and had new expectations of the consultants who were working on the village water system. They wanted to be involved in developments – not just informed. They emphasised the importance of including people and of valuing their contribution, whatever their education. They were motivated, they said, by the importance of collective benefit. 'It is always we, not me', said one of the interviewees.

As these themes unfolded out of our conversations, I found that as their former practitioner, I too had changed in relation to them, and that my change mirrored theirs in many ways.

Outsider Again

In 2000, when I returned, I stayed at the Mashabela Mission and found my experience of the village was very different. On this occasion, I related mostly to individuals, whereas before, my role had been predominantly with groups. I reflected that my 1997 experience was extraordinary in a number of ways, and that it could never happen again. This is always the case, of course – once the present has gone, it can never be recaptured – but sometimes we can return and catch glimpses of past times. We can taste the flavour of how it was then. In Mashabela in 2000, it was clear that this was not possible and I would never again relate to the village as I had.

Nong had originally brought me into the village and after the success of the first workshop, I had been formally accepted by the traditional council structure, which represented the authority of the village Chief. I had been given my village name by the Chief's brother. This was a powerful validation of my role as practitioner, by representatives at the centre of the village. Quite literally, this meant that I was included as part of the village system and that my development practice, with the values and principles that were contained within it, was then 'in relationship' with the village system. We were in an alignment and all parts of the system such as the sub villages and the women, young people, Maololo and the Learning Group were eventually connected and could exchange and influence each other and the whole.

The Learning Group became influential messengers in the system, taking messages around and facilitating the incorporation of the traditional with 'the new' as they did so. This was very clear in the Maololo process and also with the Women's Conference. Bringing the Focal Conflict Model into this reflection – the Learning Group can be seen to have had a central role in finding solutions, which expressed both the reactive fear of the conserve and the disturbing change agent motive.

Through the validations of the role of the Learning Group, the relationship between them and the Executive, and the authority given to me in my practitioner/researcher role – the village development process was firmly located in the central principle of the overall village system – in fact for a short time it formed part of the central system. This may answer some questions about how it was possible to develop the depth of learning and connection that we did, in the short time involved.

When outside agencies moved into the village at the end of 1997, they came in through the various people and networks, but failed to make strong connections with the centre or with the sub villages. They therefore never really became established. Moshate was not much involved in the new projects and therefore the messages going out to the sub villages were mixed. In effect the former coherence and resonance of development changes with the village-wide system, such as it was, broke down.

When I returned in 2000, I came back as a researcher, not a practitioner/ researcher engaged with the whole village process. I was no longer a part of the overall village system – but connected purely through individuals. The centre of the village had changed with the 'crowning' of a new Chief and a replacement of the old order with the new. The headmen and elder men were now 'out' and the young Moshate crowd was 'in'.

This explains why I felt so clearly that I could never again experience a sense of belonging to the village in the way that I had before. My experience of the village was very different and when I reflected on it, in these ways, it became clear why that was so.

8 Overview of Love Power and Learning

I chose to frame my research with the qualities of Love, Power, and Learning as a means of supporting 'person-centred' practice.

This was influenced by two key sources. The first was the writing of Md. Anisur Rahman, who argues that self-development and the need to fulfil creative potential are essential to human dignity. He offers a 'creativist' perspective as a vital alternative to a 'consumerist' view, that sees people as individual consumers or producers of goods and services, which inevitably leads to dependency and results in a primary focus on economic outcomes. By focussing on people as creative beings, the question of poverty and development outcomes become basic issues of equity. As a result, people, their essential creativity and their relationship to each other move centre stage in the development process. This brings important qualities into focus, which is missing if the primary goals are economic.

The second influence came from a workshop I attended in 1994, given by Ken Mellor, an Australian psychotherapist and meditation teacher. He introduced a model of integration that he called the Trilogy of Trilogies. Love, Power, and Wisdom were presented as qualities at a meta level; Self, Other, and Context at a positional level; and Thinking, Feeling, and Doing at a behavioural/action level. He suggested the three layers of trilogies could overlap, exchange, and complement each other.

LOVE	POWER	WISDOM	meta layer
SELF	OTHER	CONTEXT	positional layer
THINKING	FEELING	DOING	behavioural layer

In presenting the model, Ken Mellor was promoting the value of personal integration and balance. Within this, he presented the meta trilogy as having a specifically spiritual flavour, with Love, Power and Wisdom as overarching qualities that could be seen as transcending the ordinary. It was as if these qualities might be viewed as filters (already naturally present) that when unobstructed, could spread their 'light' over the process.

I became interested in using the meta qualities as a means of guiding and shaping my work. I replaced Wisdom with Learning, as this seemed a lot more relevant. It also linked directly with Md. Anisur Rahman's notions of people as creative beings.

When I planned the South African research, I used Love, Power, and Learning to frame the proposal. I wanted to explore whether they stood up to being applied to development practice in a much tougher physical environment.

I shall briefly introduce and define each quality in the context of development and then return to look at what can be learnt from using Love, Power, and Learning to reflect on the Mashabela intervention. I use capital letters throughout this section when referring to the meta qualities.

Love

Love is not a quality usually applied to development – nor is it a word to use easily in this sort of context. It is often used very widely and loosely to mean all sorts of things – so it is important to describe it carefully here.

We tend to talk least about what touches us most deeply and language often debases the very preciousness of an experience. As soon as we try to use words to describe something that is intrinsically experiential, qualitative and personal, we start to have difficulties. We find it hard to describe and then when we try, we find that the experience itself gets lost or changed in our attempts to articulate it.

We restrict most talk of love to romantic love – or parental love for a child. We tend to keep words of 'love' within the private spheres of feeling and emotional experience, usually well away from the public domain of organisations and communities. There is, after all, much in public life which is far from loveable!

But as MJ Makamatleng, headmaster of one of the Mashabela secondary schools, said:

> 'When we first talked about love in workshops I thought it was the love between a girl and a boy. What kind of love is this?! I listened with surprise – and then it came to me very simply, that this love was co-operation and accepting other people. It was not new – but in the context of development, love was new. The feelings were already there'.

Let us explore what Love might offer in the context of development.

It relates to a shared connection between people that is able to express qualities of openness, regard, trust, warmth, interest, mutuality and sensitivity. It might be said to be a response to the natural goodness that exists in people. In the exchange and flow of Love, that is not erotic or romantic, positive regard, acceptance, and respect have strong roles to play.

Growth – Promoting Relationships

Carl Rogers[11], the distinguished psychiatrist and founder of the 'person-centred' approach in counselling and psychotherapy, looked at the therapeutic relationship and asked some important questions. He found evidence that threw light on the attitudes of a 'helping person' which made their relationships growth-promoting or growth-inhibiting. Those that promoted growth tended to be warm, accepting and equalitarian. The 'helper' was likely to be expressive and respectful of herself and others. Those being helped tended to develop relationships with the 'helper' in which they experienced trust and confidence. Successful relationships were closely associated with strong and growing mutual liking and respect between client and counsellor.

Rogers asked how we can create helping relationships with those that we work with that facilitate growth. He posed a number of important questions:

- 'Can I **be** in some way which will be perceived by others as trustworthy, dependable, or consistent in some deep sense?'

- 'Can I let myself experience positive attitudes toward this other person – attitudes of warmth, caring, liking, interest and respect?'

- 'Can I let myself enter into the world of his feelings and personal meanings and see these as he does?' – (losing all desire to judge?)

- 'Can I be expressive enough as a person that what I am will be communicated (to others) unambiguously?'

In reflecting on these questions, Rogers suggests that what is involved here entails more than mere actions. It has to include a level of personal congruence on the part of the 'helper' that goes into the essence who s/he is, demonstrating an integrity of actions with intentions and awareness. It has to imply wholeness.

*'I **can** be whatever I deeply am.'*[11]

Rogers' questions have relevance to work in development. We do not want to build therapeutic relationships with those with whom we work, but if we accept Md. Anisur Rahman's ideas of people as creative beings, then as development practitioners, it is important that we reflect on the qualities that we bring to our development relationships. This is an area that often gets overlooked. In most development and community work training, the focus is on developing the 'hard' skills of expertise, not the 'soft' ones of process, connection and people-centred enabling.

For me, Rogers' questions relate closely to qualities of Love. To suggest that we need to love the people we work with is contentious and might be interpreted as patronising, or even manipulative. But if we were to be simple and genuine here – we might speak of developing kindness, understanding, empathy, and above all respect, acceptance and openness. It is not the same as personal love – of course not – nor should it be – but in the flow between people engaged in essential development that is creative and has important potential for the future, is it so strange for us to use our hearts in how we connect with others and work with them?

'Where intellect and emotion clash, the heart often has the greater wisdom.'[12]

In the village of Mashabela, warm connections were evident amongst the women and amongst the men, on occasions. And sometimes, I felt an open warmth in the way that village people connected to me, and I to them. Connection is usually about flow and exchange. After living in Africa, I came to understand much better, the place of Love in development – and learnt some of this directly from the people of Mashabela. It is not so surprising that I found it easier to talk with local people about Love in development in a South African village, than I had in a council estate in the North.

Love in Mashabela was referred to, by the villagers, in relation to:

- connecting with people in a way that built trust, safety and learning

- accepting others, and being prepared to listen to them and hear their ideas, whatever or whoever they were

- co-operating with people, working with you to achieve a common goal that benefits everyone

Power

Power is a term often used in relation to development, in the context of political action and theory. Because of this, it might seem a lot less controversial to include than love. After all, it is the inequalities of power and opportunity that cause oppression and exclusion – and it is these factors that are at the root of most development needs. But in which case, what sort of Power is suggested here as a meta quality?

Definitions of Power

Indeed, what is power? Steven Lukes,[13] a sociologist from Balliol College, Oxford, presents three views. In the first, one dimensional view, power and influence tend to be used interchangeably. Power here involves behaviour and/or decision making, where there is an overt conflict of interests between groups of people. In the second, the two dimensional view, the critics of the first view argue for the inclusion of 'bias' and include all forms of successful control by A over B including force and coercion. So when issues are excluded by one group that might be in the interests of another, this would be included as power.

The three dimensional view takes the analysis of power a good bit further, by showing that control can be exercised in many ways, which may or (importantly) may not involve actual conflict. Lukes suggests that 'the most effective and insidious use of power is to prevent conflict arising in the first place' by whatever means, even if those being excluded are not aware of their interests.

This last view has important applications to development. As ordinary people involved in the process of development develop their conscious awareness of the way their interests are being excluded, they then start to act collectively to 'pool' their available influence for change. However, exclusion is mirrored inside communities as well, when groups of people (eg. the women) are marginalised by more powerful others (eg. the men).

Power as a Property of the Group

Hannah Arendt, a German Jewish political theorist, who wrote after the Second World War, made a valuable contribution to this discussion. She saw power 'as the property of a group' (not of individuals), which only existed when the group came together. Once the group dispersed, the power disappeared. 'Power springs up whenever people get together and act in concert, but it derives its legitimacy from the initial getting together, rather than from any action that may follow'[14].

This might link with the discussion of Love, above, and Learning, below, when ordinary people make connections that are based on trust, mutual acceptance and respect, openness and co-operation.

> *'Power is actualised only where word and deed have not parted company, where words are not empty and deeds not brutal, where words are not used to veil intentions but to disclose realities, and deeds are not used to violate and destroy but to establish relations and create new realities'.*[14]

As Arendt suggests, when these connections form, people find the confidence to act and to speak their own truths. They begin to feel able to participate and become aware of perspectives relating to their experience that are new and may affect them deeply. They start to realise their own potential to be powerful and effect change.

This relates to Ubuntu – a form of African humanism – which suggests that a person is only a person through her relation to others. Ubuntu is not so much a form of humanism in the 'Western' sense, which tends to see people primarily as material consumers, but leans towards a more African sense of balance that includes both the material and the spiritual. Archbishop Desmond Tutu has a strong perspective of Ubuntu that has flavours in common with Md. Anisur Rahman's view of development as 'creativist' or 'consumerist'.

> *'In the African Weltanschauung, a person is not basically an independent solitary entity. A person is human precisely in being enveloped in the community of other human beings, in being caught up in the bundle of life. To be is to participate. The summum bonum here is not independence but sharing, interdependence.'*[15]

For Tutu, Ubuntu is the environment of vulnerability, i.e. a set of relationships in which people are able to recognise that their humanity is bound up in the other's. The African Xhosa expression is not easy to translate 'Umuntu ngumuntu ngabanye bantu'. One way is to say that 'we are fully human because we are in community. And it is only in community that justice can be done to individuals'.[16]

> *'I am because we are, and since we are, therefore I am.'*[17]

Empowerment

In development, the term 'empowerment' is often used in ways which can be problematic. It is easily misunderstood to imply that someone 'empowers' someone else.

If empowerment is seen as an activity similar to facilitation – where the process itself releases the already existent potential of people to participate as creative beings – then it ceases to be others who empower. It is the process which empowers.

Paulo Freire, the Brazilian father of community development and community education used the term 'empowerment' without apology and in recognition of the power of collaboration in the collective group.

> '*Empowerment is a consequence of liberatory learning. Power is not given, but created within the emerging praxis in which co-learners are engaged. For poor and dispossessed people, strength is in numbers and social change is accomplished in unity. Power is shared, not the power of a few who improve themselves at the expense of others, but the power of the many who find strength and purpose in a common vision.*'[18]

Human Capital

It is important to recognise how radically different this approach is to that in which people are the objects of sympathy and seen as 'poor' or as 'victims' who need help. Indeed if people are the recipients of programmes that are focussed on alleviating poverty, there is little or no space for them to be respected as people with knowledge, dignity and experience, either in potential or in a realised way. Economic development that has little or no people-centred process, with goals that are determined outside, '*dis*-empowers', inhibits learning and encourages dependency.

Recent literature on 'human capital' in many ways emphasises people's productive and economic potential. But by using a broader lens that includes the capacity of humans to learn and achieve outcomes that are both material and non-material, human capital can be seen more significantly to relate to freedom and dignity. Amartya Sen, Winner of the 1998 Nobel Prize in Economic Science, has an influential and very human approach to economics.

> '*The acknowledgement of the role of human qualities in promoting and sustaining economic growth – momentous as it is – tell us nothing about why economic growth is sought in the first place. If, instead, the focus is, ultimately, on the expansion of human freedom to live the kind of lives that people have reason to value, the role of economic growth in expanding these*

opportunities has to be integrated into that more foundational understanding of the process of development as the expansion of human capability to lead more worthwhile and more free lives.'[19]

Indeed, Robert Putnam, who coined the term 'human capital' in 'Bowling Alone',[20] emphasises the potential power in the interaction between people that enables them to build communities, commit themselves to each other, and themselves weave together the essentials of their society. So, if Power is included in the perspective of human ability to connect, learn and act together in a process of collective and mutual benefit – and this potential is acknowledged as a tremendous social and development asset – then it can be seen that the flavour of the development process is transformed.

Personal Awareness

Another aspect of Power relates to the awareness of the practitioner and of the people she works with.

Most people are only partially aware in an ordinary sense, most of the time. Indeed, in the fog of the automatic, we miss a lot of detail about the processes and experiences that we are involved in. We may be there in our physical bodies but often, our minds are elsewhere.

If we are lost in thinking, as we are most of the time, and at the mercy of our habitual reactions, it takes practice and commitment to become aware in everyday life, so that we can be fully involved with what we are doing.

As development practitioners, I suggest that the clarity of our awareness is a vital quality to bring to our practice. It includes the preparedness to listen more than to talk; to be really present with each person and in each situation.

Martin Buber, a Jewish teacher and significant thinker in the education world of the last century, suggested that there are three forms of dialogue:

'There is genuine dialogue – no matter whether spoken or silent – where each of the participants really has in mind the other or others in their present and particular being and turns to them with the intention of establishing a living mutual relation between himself and them. There is technical dialogue, which is prompted solely by the need of objective understanding. And there is monologue disguised as dialogue, in which two or more men, meeting in space, speak each with himself in strangely tortuous and circuitous ways and yet imagine they have escaped the torment of being thrown back on their own resources.'[21]

Being genuinely and fully present with others involves attention that is not fixed or rigid and a commitment to be relaxed and open, in a way that avoids being casual or sloppy. Here we are talking, as Carl Rogers did, about **being** with people (and with ourselves) in the mutual process of development. There is, then, an opportunity to be skilful in ways that may surprise. When the practitioner herself 'gets out of the way', the process can manifest an organic spontaneity, offering powerful insights to those involved.

To conclude – the meta quality of Power relates to Md. Anisur Rahman's notion of people as creative beings. It connects to the collective within 'Ubuntu', which needs the relationship with 'other' to acknowledge the presence of 'self'. This concept of Power transcends political concepts that are based on coercion, force or manipulation. It is based instead within the aware presence of individuals and in the resonance, connection and mutuality of the group. Power thus can be viewed as the inherent capacity to come together and act for a common good.

'To love him as myself, and to do to all men, as I would they should do to me.'[22]

Learning

Learning is an uncontentious term to apply to development. It is surely the central building block, without which development has not really taken place. There may be accepted core principles and processes, but we always have to discover them for ourselves through our own experience. This is at the heart of personal learning.

According to John Heron,[23] there are three forms of knowing: propositional knowing or *knowing about*; experiential knowing or *knowing by encounter*; and *knowing how to*, which involves skills and abilities. Translated into learning, we might describe these as learning with your head, your heart and your hands.

Experiential learning is potentially 'transformational' – transforming attitudes and behaviour in relation to self, others and context. It is at the heart of the intervention described in this book.

Experiential learning relates closely to action. People learn far more from **doing** things themselves and with others like them, than they do through being taught about something. Indeed, those doing the teaching invariably learn more about the subject than those that they teach. People know much more than they think they do (especially when learning from experience), and when they attempt to apply their learning and experiment alongside their peers, and then reflect and discuss what happened, their learning is likely to be rich and well remembered.

Sometimes in these sorts of situations, people experience 'light bulb' learning, when a number of things come together and make sense with a new clarity. Then, learning results in important new behaviours that probably relate to an increased sense of personal power and authenticity. Once these are practiced and incorporated, the newness of the learning is forgotten, and they become part of the repertoire of that individual's role, and behaviour.

I referred to Kolb's action learning cycle earlier in this chapter and also to the African House Model, which describes the enabling conditions needed for individuals to be able to start learning 'experientially'.

The true meta quality of learning is Wisdom, and in a development context Learning is difficult to differentiate from 'ordinary' learning – as it rests at the foundation of personal and collective processes for change, creativity and transformation.

Love, Power and Learning

It is sometimes hard to separate the three qualities. As described here they often overlap and interconnect. Without Love, Power is not a transforming quality – but risks becoming another force that coerces or excludes. Without Power, Love might lose its edge and risk becoming sentimental and self-serving. With mutuality and interconnection, it becomes transformative. Learning brings a certain balance and focus – and importantly an outcome orientation – which often involves the other two.

Paulo Freire, guided by a strong commitment to principles, put social transformation at the root of his teaching. He never tired of repeating that 'before learning anything, a person must first read his/her world'.[24] He argued that any learning that ignores racism, sexism, and all forms of oppression at the same time is supporting the *status quo* – and limiting the expansion of human consciousness and blocking social action for change.

Martin Buber saw encounter and awareness to be central to who we are, how we learn and develop.

'As we live, we grow and our beliefs change. They must change. So I think we should live with this constant discovery. We should be open to this adventure in heightened awareness of living. We should stake our whole existence on our willingness to explore and experience.'[25]

9 Transforming Moments

Having examined the stages of the intervention, one by one, and explored the meta qualities that framed my research and guided my practice, I now want to draw out the times when Love, Power and Learning lit up the whole development process.

The first occasion was in the first workshop, when the participants imagined that everyone had a tap in their yard and was turning it on, feeling the cold water on their hands, hearing the splash in the bucket, and seeing their neighbour doing the same thing. People laughed out loud, smiling at each other. There was bright active energy in the dark classroom, and a sense of strong connection and positive outlook that did not immediately fade. For a few moments, everyone believed that it was possible to work together to get water.

On another occasion, at the end of the large Maololo village meeting, when people were walking back to their homes, a group from the Learning Group and the Maololo planning group were standing together, expressing pleasure at how well it had all gone. We were watching the bright colours of all the people walking away from the school – and felt an intense sense of connection and joy, satisfaction at the success of the meeting, optimism at what was possible, and relief now it was over.

Again in Maololo, at the second meeting, when the women announced their decision to dig out the well, the dark schoolroom almost seemed to light up with the energy of their courage and determination. It was an intense moment of joy, excitement, and optimism that was very infectious – and even world-weary Bob, the water engineer, was strongly affected.

At the women's conference, the atmosphere in the room was so intense at times, it seemed that the roof might fly off. It is true that there was a lot of noise, from the drumming, singing, and dancing – but it was more than that. There was a powerful sense of connection between the women that was expressed in joy and celebration of being together. Anything seemed possible and all the difficulties melted away.

All these occasions and others like them have conditions in common. You could say that they are simply moments of high energy, when things had gone well and people were able to relax into enjoying and affirming what they had achieved. It is true that many of them have that flavour – but there was also a strong sense of connection between people, and increased confidence, and creativity.

These moments (and sometimes they last longer) are important times of spontaneity. They have strong impact, and allow people to open in ways that can touch them deeply. The learning insight is a glimpse of gold, and with it comes a warm sense of connection with others, and confidence, and optimism within the group.

These moments cannot be planned. There are ingredients and there are conditions that need to be present – but even then, just as when baking a favourite cake, you can follow the same recipe and even use identical ingredients, but still find the cake is different every time.

In Mashabela, we had moments of gold that touched us all, and offered us learning that broke down barriers, long in place – and if only for moments, allowed us to come face to face with each other and who we are.

> *'Not Christian or Jew or Muslim, nor Hindu, Buddhist, sufi, or zen. Not any religion or cultural system. I am not from the East or the West, nor out of the ocean or up from the ground, not natural or ethereal, not composed of elements at all. I do not exist, am not an entity in this world or the next, did not descend from Adam or Eve or any origin story. My place is placeless, a trace of the traceless. Neither body or soul. I belong to the beloved, have seen the two worlds as one and that one call to and know, first, last, outer, inner, only that breath, breathing human being.'*
>
> Rumi[26]

Nong Makola

My name is Nong John Makola. I am 48 years old and married to Segapi. We have five children – four girls Delia, Nandi, Ouma and Seponka and one young boy called Sebutswa

I have been unemployed for some time. I used to work in Johannesburg as a clerk for Avis. I was there for 12 years.

I have been involved in development for many years and am currently studying (part time) for a Diploma in Development and Leadership Management in Pietersburg.

I worked closely with Manyaku, when she was here with us and I was a member of the Learning Group. I have acted as the village Community Development Worker for some years. Before that, I was chairperson of the Mashabela Development Forum.

I don't know if this happens to other people, but for me love comes first in development. I really love people and I also practice love in my own house. Since I've been involved in development, I think I've loved my children more — my wife much more than ever before. I think it is because I am learning about people — so now I take notice of everything that happens next to me. I try to work on everything that I see and appreciate what is good.

In our culture we respect our ancestors. We pray to them. We don't regard them as God but we do respect them. They have put down examples of the standard that we must adhere to. We feel that we have an obligation to fulfil, to respect old people, to do good to others in the hope that God will give more. If I see somebody being miserable, I feel I want to help that somebody — to get them out of that trouble — because it could be me.

You know who you are, because other people put you where you belong. If you are a good somebody, they will really respect you and if you have good qualities they will vote you into a leadership position. If you are bad, the people will turn away from you.

I approach what I want to do with optimism. I become convinced that it will work. Before, my participation in workshops and meetings — and talking informally to people — was low. If you are not empowered, you doubt yourself. You get shy and are afraid to make mistakes. I am not afraid any more. I know I am learning because I am making mistakes.

I wish I could do more to empower others. There are few, who are willing to work with me. We have a natural disease here — which is a tendency for people to think that the only capable people in this village are teachers. They don't really take notice of people in other studies or fields. I would like to be running workshops at village level — doing much more.

I doubt if we all understand empowerment the same way. Some would just take it as feeding someone with knowledge — then you find that person is not doing anything. To me empowerment goes hand in glove with participation and taking action.

I think the way I worked with Manyaku was empowering. We used to sit down and discuss what we were going to do. Where I didn't understand, I could ask her to explain the concepts further. Then we stood up and went and did the things together and even evaluated what we had done to check it has made some differences. I think I got it the right way.

Bringing the village together was the best thing that we did. I tell you, it even saved this village. I think we could have seen something like a civil war, if it was not because of our involvement after the death of the chief. The way we settled the appointment of the young queen and the way we negotiated for her salary, we did it professionally, I think. We might have had a lot of people oppose the queen – and say 'Let us appoint another man in the place of the chief'. The provincial government allows women to be chiefs now, but I know it is not happening in other villages. We managed to bring the relevant people together and talk to the government and in the end the MDC (Mashabela Development Council) and the old men of the Royal Kraal agreed to appoint the queen.

I feel young when I learn a lot. I feel like I have a lot of knowledge and I need a lot of time to implement it. Mentally it extends your days in life. Now I am 48, I wish I could live for 20 years longer and then I could make a lot of changes in my village. I would live longer so that I could make more.

My message to people about development:

'If I was teaching someone about development who knew very little – the first thing I would try to do, is to make that person feel great and knowledgeable. He is a person. He has the skills. He or she has wisdom. I would really show appreciation of what that person knows and help to make her aware.'

 FOUR

The Principles

May what I do flow from me like a river,
no forcing and no holding back,
the way it is with children.
Then in these swelling and ebbing currents,
these deepening tides moving out, returning,
I will sing you as no one ever has,
streaming through widening channels into the
open sea.

Rainer Maria Rilke[1]

The goals of many development interventions are prescribed before they begin, by specified measurable outcomes, formulated by people who usually have no direct involvement in the development process. The outcomes dictate the focus, and usually result in limiting the potential for authentic people-centred development.

The process that involves people in coming together to work on their own agendas has the power within it to build confidence and trust in those who lack both. This is one of the most effective ways for people to discover themselves and realise their own capacity to change their lives for the better.

It is often tempting to imagine that there are ways of fixing problems by prescribing specific standard methods. Participation is one such mirage.

'Participation matters — not only as a means of improving development effectiveness...but as a key to long term sustainability and leverage'. [2]

In the interests of trying to promote good practice, it is easy to oversimplify — and by doing so, risk missing what has real meaning. All too often, participatory development results in the creation of new elites, who become more powerful it is true, but then in turn exclude those they leave behind, in the same way that they were once marginalised and excluded by others.

As Arnstein's ladder of participation[3] demonstrates, participatory approaches come in many forms, and skill, experience, and integrity are needed to facilitate processes that genuinely and appropriately involve, include and develop.

There is no one right way of 'doing' development, and it seems to me that as practitioner, the best I can do is to continue to question, reflect, renew my intention and work at the uncomfortable 'edges' of my practice.

This chapter brings together the principles drawn down from the learning of the previous chapter. Five central themes act as guiding signposts that point out my pathway of practice, with sub-headings that give a chance to see the landscape in more detail. Over time, it may be that some of the detailed headings will change with the advent of new understandings, but the central principles will endure, as they are grounded in overarching qualities that are in themselves transforming.

Local People are the Experts in their Own Lives

- Being Aware of Difference – Working with Diversity
- We Not Me

Love – Building Connection, Developing Trust

- Including the Excluded – Honouring Difference
- Working with Heart and Mind

Power – Being Present

- Grounded in Experience
- Narrowing the Focus Down – Widening the Attention Out
- Remembering the Big Picture
- Trusting the Process
- Focusing on the Positive
- Learning from Outcomes

Learning – Is Mutual

- Going Round the Circle Together

- Walking in the Shoes of Others
- Walking Round the Tree
- Turning Towards
- Developing the Practitioner Too

Aligning with Intention – Working with Congruence

- Working with the Basic Goodness of People
- Not So Much Building Capacity – As Helping to Dismantle the Barriers
- Walking the Talk
- Maintaining the Vehicle
- Resonating Values

▌ Local People are the Experts in their Own Lives

This seems to be a good place to start. People who live in poverty lack the resources and opportunity to improve the quality of their lives. Marginalised, they do not have the power to make choices about the things that matter to them. However, they know about themselves and their communities, and they do have the potential to develop their skills and their learning. With respect, support, opportunity and information, they are the best people to be involved in working to change their communities and their own lives.

In general, they often lack:

- the confidence to say what they know
- the opportunity to get involved
- experience of effective working together and
- understanding of the context, and the way the system works

All these 'lacks' combine to undermine their knowledge, creativity and dignity, which affects every aspect of their well-being.

Most people living in disadvantaged areas do not feel competent or capable of making decisions about their own communities. Decisions are usually made without them. When the so-called experts arrive, in the guise of development workers, business leaders, doctors, water engineers, regeneration consultants, and so on – local people easily feel disempowered, reinforcing their sense of inadequacy and lack of confidence.

However, local people *are* the experts in their own lives. They are the only ones with personal and intimate knowledge of an area. It is only they, who have the capacity to transform their experience from feeling excluded, dependent, or marginalised to feeling confident and positively creative. It is only they who can come together with others like them, to improve the quality of their lives. If others attempt to do it for them, the outcomes are different and the opportunities for local people to learn and develop are lost.

A first important step can be made by genuinely respecting and affirming their knowledge and skills. They can then begin to believe in their own expertise and assert their right to be involved. This may sound simple, but if it is done genuinely and followed through congruently, it can make a significant impact. Affirming local people as the experts in their own lives is the basis of respecting them.

Being Aware of Difference – Working with Diversity

In many communities and projects, the development practitioner, whatever her actual job title, comes from a different race, area, or class to local people. This may not always be the case, but even those who have started out as local activists will have changed through their experience and/or training.

Being aware of the impact of inequality and working skilfully with diversity and local culture, is at the heart of all development practice. It is not easy and there are no simple formulas. Much depends on the genuine intention of the practitioner to be aware of the factors that oppress, and be open to learn about herself and the people with whom she is working. 'Valuing difference' could become yet another stock phrase, and mean little, unless translated into action that comes from the heart, not just the intellect.

Gathering local information, mapping, and understanding the history and conditions of an area are important first steps, which offer an opportunity for the culture to show itself, and for stories and experiences to be told. If local people are the experts in their community, outsiders can demonstrate their intention to respect difference by listening, looking, and learning when they first arrive. This is essential practice that helps local people to articulate their own condition and make meaning of their own lives. This is not the time for generating solutions or sharing ideas, which will immediately put the power back with the practitioner, but for showing and telling, listening and connecting.

We Not Me

As mentioned earlier, there is a risk in the development process that the people who become empowered use their influence unwisely, to build themselves up, rather than work to benefit the community, group, or project as a whole. The development process should certainly increase the confidence of group members, but at the same time bring through outcomes that benefit the wider community.

An exploration of values is an important part of the development process. It is not a one-off exercise to identify them and then be done with it, but a developing thread that is woven into every aspect of the work. Values are not static – they develop over time and experience.

The values of including the excluded and honouring difference are core tools in the development process. If there is acceptance within the group that all contributions are valuable, then a culture is nurtured that embeds *that* value into practice. If something is stated as being important, but not modelled in the group, a lack of congruence shows up immediately, which inevitably undermines the whole process.

Development interventions are not designed to produce outcomes that benefit particular individuals, although there is often potential for great individual benefit. It is better that development focuses on collective action taken on behalf of the individual and others like you – your neighbours, family members, friends, and fellow human beings, experiencing a similar condition to you. Then, if collective benefit is achieved and sustained, it will invariably involve the energy and activity of those most affected – with outside consultants and practitioners, who also benefit from the process in a number of ways, working *with* them, but *not* for them.

2 Love – Building Connection, Developing Trust

It is a challenge to express softness in the world. It is usually kept for the private and domestic spheres that women predominantly inhabit. In the public, predominantly male world of policy and practice, intellectual precision and clear focus are most valued.

However the connections that exist in society, which are rich in emotion, are the vital pulse in the lifeblood of communities. Those, whose connections have broken down, can no longer function as organic entities. Most communities are only partially connected, with some parts completely excluded. Some communities appear connected, but on closer investigation have deep rifts, which include some and exclude others. A community is more than a geographical area – it is a connection linking people who have interests, history, values, conditions and experiences in common, and who have the potential to articulate a shared meaning and learn out of their common experience. In a sense, a community is an organism in its own right – in which the individual parts have the potential to interconnect, and come into synergy. The whole is more than the sum of its parts – and people have to connect, build trust, and learn to work together, if they are to make profound changes in their community.

Even though the conflicts and difficulties of some communities appear to be intractable, slowly, connections can be built, if there is commitment, skill and patience to bring people together to talk, listen and share experiences. One place to start is by developing structures that are explicit and open, and by taking every opportunity to involve people in planning how things will evolve. This takes time.

It is a subtle undertaking to keep things clear and explicit, whilst leaving open as much space as possible for people to participate. Too much structure and propping up of the process can lead to dependency. Not enough can result in fear, and the loss of a sense of trust and safety, which will reduce participation and connection. All the way through, awareness is needed to carefully balance the scales.

Including the Excluded – Honouring Difference

When excluded parts of the community are involved in a shared process, a capacity for inclusion develops. It gets easier to involve others, who were formerly excluded, as those at the centre begin to experience the benefits. When the move to include gets stuck or is challenged, if connection and trust building is an embedded value in the intervention, the difficulties and issues of difference can be made explicit and 'public' – and can then be worked with, if conditions support this. New connections change power imbalances, even if albeit subtly. It can be a slow process, but as layer on layer is worked with, so opportunities grow to nurture co-operation and consolidate participation. These are the roots of peaceful communities, where people can navigate changing patterns through including and respecting others.

There is a dynamic power in connections that are forged between people, based on a shared, collectively defined purpose. People can experience being part of a whole that is more than just the combination of their individual interests. Positive intent combines with experience to produce learning that transforms and benefits others, not just self. When connections are formed between networks/groups of people that share a central purpose, a resonance can result that has potential to greatly benefit the whole. This is the way of profound participation, where a change in one part affects and changes all.

Working with Heart and Mind

If we see our development work as a craft, similar to that of the midwife, in which the skills are immensely complex and demand great integrity and intention, then how can we imagine we can do it without kindness and the qualities of heart? The mind and the intellect are vital tools to the practitioner, but the thinking mind is not enough. It only allows for the coolness of analysis and problem-solving. The way of working with heart as well as mind is crucial for really skilful practice. It allows space for kindness and compassion based on an appreciation of fellow humans. The heart of the practitioner is her key tool to understand the issues for local people and connect with them in a way that fully appreciates their impact. This is a difficult area since 'professionalism' is all too often seen to rely on cool objectivity. A balance is obviously needed that includes appropriate boundaries between local people and those who work with them – but also allows space for a kind heart and a reflexive, sensitive personal practice.

However, there is no prescription that dictates how this can be done. To stay with the midwife metaphor, she is not responsible for the weight of the baby at the birth, or the colour of the baby's eyes, or its gender. She does have immense responsibility for the process of birth, for which she needs years of training and supervision – and for which she needs to keep up to date with current good practice. Like the midwife, our role as practitioners is to nurture the development process with great care, being aware of the stages of development as best we can, to guard and protect against potential risk where possible. But like the midwife we must intervene as little as possible, just enough to enable local people to come together and give birth to their collective experience of community, learning, and connection.

3 Power – Being Present

There have been many references to 'being present' and aware. As practitioners, trying to facilitate groups and processes, it is vital that we are fully present. So often we are not – and by only partially paying attention, we miss a great deal. The people we work with are aware (at some level) the moment our attention wanders. This inevitably gives a negative message to them about their value, and greatly detracts from our ability to respond fully to what is happening.

Grounded In Experience

Being present and aware is immensely powerful – in a beneficial way – and ultimately is the essence of what it is to be authentic. Although I have presented this as a separate heading, it links strongly to professional integrity and personal intention (see below). Awareness – being centred in our experience – is all we have with which to align our actions with our intention. Then we know whether or not we have behaved in ways that fit our values.

Being grounded is infectious. It is said that the most grounded person in a group is also the most resourceful, predictable, and empowering. All of us are grounded and aware to some extent, but by deliberately paying attention and noticing sensations, thoughts, and emotions, we can apparently increase our awareness or remove some of the obstacles to it.

Psychotherapists say that the issues of their clients often mirror their own. This is so with development practitioners too – if we are aware. The world has a habit of reflecting me back to myself. What work am I doing with others that I need to do on myself? What do I feel when I am with this group? Is the sensation or experience entirely mine? Or is it reflected through a parallel process in the group? (It will invariably be both.)

Narrowing the Focus Down– Widening the Attention Out

When we are starting out in development work, as in any other practice, we need definition and guidance. We are introduced to methods and processes which we follow as best we can. As our experience and understanding grows, we refine our learning and start to make the work more truly our own. There are times when our practice seems to get more complicated and involved, and other rarer times when things appear wonderfully simple and clear.

It seems that practice and research involve an ongoing process of narrowing and widening, like the beam of a torch. Sometimes we go so wide that a sense of specific focus or definition is almost lost – and sometimes we become so focussed and single pointed that there is no longer much awareness of the wider context at all. Neither is wrong. But as these processes occur, it is helpful to know where we are, to keep us on track – so that we know whether our development is widening to incorporate new ideas or refining to clarify existing ones. Both will take place, but awareness is needed to bring the learning through and make the process explicit.

Remembering the Big Picture

This highlights the importance of keeping some attention on the development context. It is easily forgotten in the narrow focus of whatever is currently demanding attention or causing problems. Without information about the context and attention to it – it is impossible to fully understand the system in which the development is operating, or to anticipate how the system can help or might hinder the development. It is also worth remembering that different aspects of the system will mirror the rest – so there may be much that is happening 'outside' in the wider context that might give guidance about how to work 'inside' the development process.

Trusting the Process

These references to awareness and being present might be misinterpreted to suggest that development practice involves a need to control the process. Quite the reverse is true. If centred and grounded in experience and, as far as possible, present in the moment, the practitioner has the option of letting go of 'doing' and trusting the process to take care of itself – even if she has no idea where it will go. This is difficult to write about, since this 'knowing' depends on context, reflection, personal experience and something akin to hunch or intuition. It involves a readiness to simply be present, to honour the process and support and trust what is happening, wherever it might go.

Sometimes, this might be in response to apparent chaos and confusion, which if left, may find its own creative expression, and resolve in learning that is more profound than anything that could be planned. This is not the same as a *laissez faire* approach, which just leaves people to sink or swim without support – far from it. It involves courage and a preparedness to take risks that are grounded in an essential trust of people and process.

> *'There is a way between voice and presence*
> *Where information flows*
> *In disciplined silence it opens.*
> *With wandering talk it closes.'*[4]

It is in our nature to be powerful – not in order to use that power *over* others – but to find that power *with* others and use it for a common benefit. Sometimes, power needs to be expressed through silence that holds a wide openness of 'don't know'. All too often we fill up the spaces with our knowing conceptual minds, and control the moment – removing the potential for spontaneity and magic to come through.

> *'Our deepest fear is not that we are inadequate. Our deepest fear is that we are powerful beyond measure. It is our light, not our darkness that most frightens us. We ask ourselves, "Who am I to be brilliant, gorgeous, talented, fabulous?" Actually, who are you not to be?…Your playing small does not serve the world…We are all meant to shine, as children do…And as we let*

our own light shine, we unconsciously give other people permission to do the same. As we are liberated from our own fear, our presence automatically liberates others.'[5]

Focussing on the Positive

The condition of marginalised people often seems hopeless. There is so much individual and collective suffering that it is hard to comprehend – and hard to stay with, emotionally. If predictive outcomes were considered logically, much development would never start. However we are not working with logic, but with people, their lives and opportunities. A positive focus is needed to work with what is possible. Generating optimistic aspirations that are impossible to realise is unethical and unskilful – but working only with struggle and difficulty is futile.

There are no easy answers or quick fixes to this dichotomy – but even in the midst of the most tragic and ghastly situations, there are examples of inspiring behaviour of great wonder and beauty.

Responsible ways of working with what is possible, through envisaging what is wanted and needed, is a powerful and effective way for people to set positive goals, rather than remain locked in despair or dependency. By inviting them to identify and then experience their own goals (like imagining, feeling, and hearing the water flowing from the tap in the yard), whilst staying 'real' and grounded in the present, enables them to be aware of what action they need to take, to achieve their goals. It also helps them to feel more optimistic and competent. The process brings future fantasy into the present as a tool to help people to create positive visions.

However it is important that these images are not held on to rigidly, and that small steps are taken to ground what is real. If goals become fixed and people start to grasp the vision too tightly, the value of the process is lost.

Learning from Outcomes

Outcomes are unpredictable. This is so obvious that it hardly needs saying. But we can sometimes become so fixed on an idea of what would be best that we fail to see that what we have is useful in its own way – it may even be better than what we hoped for in the first place – and it certainly offers us learning if we are open to it.

Anyway whatever the outcome, how can we accurately judge what is best? At the end of the day, much has to be left to processes over which we have little or no control. If we have invested our skills and energy in supporting people in a development process that is as widely owned as possible by the people we work with – it is inappropriate and unwise to take more than our fair share of responsibility. I am not suggesting this lightly, but as practitioners, if we have committed to our intention, and developed our practice with integrity and awareness – all we can then do is review and reflect to learn lessons for the future.

4 Learning Is Mutual

Learning is the key focus of people-centred development – and is crucially important even where development involves practical infrastructure goals. It is learning that enables development to be sustainable and we work to support people to learn about themselves and their communities of interest, so that they can live and sustain healthy lives of dignity and connection.

The process involves the learning of the practitioner as much as the local people. They are developing and learning about themselves, as she too is involved in learning and changing her understanding of herself alongside them. This mutual process of learning side by side is enriching to the whole, and all those involved in it.

Going Round the Circle Together

Development learning is predominantly focussed on experience rather than on facts or theories. It involves people in sharing and delving into their lives. They discover things that they already knew, and in the discovery, understand them differently and at a greater depth. As they make these discoveries, often with others like them, they start to change the way they see themselves, and begin to walk on a path of greater confidence and security. Even though this process is often collective, it can start to remove the obstacles that stand in the way of personal dignity, accumulated through societal oppression and exclusion. One person's learning often opens the doors for others – and as each learns, they start to understand differences and similarities between themselves and others like them.

It is helpful to remember the need to 'go around' the learning circle several times in order to integrate and apply new learning behaviour. This is as true for the practitioner as it is for the people she is working with. A mutually shared learning process can be rich – and has a potency that can dramatically nurture personal development. Without a mutuality in this process, the learning can easily be seen as one person (the practitioner) doing something for others – and thereby reinforcing all the inequalities that oppress, diminish and foster dependency.

Standing in the Shoes of Others

There are different styles and schools of development learning that offer variations on the same tune of creativity, personal learning, and spontaneity. One such approach, Sociodrama, came out of Moreno's Psychodrama method. This invites people to explore the system they are in and 'stand in the shoes of' others, to gain new understanding of their own condition. It allows them to expand their experience of how they thought things were, and develop new knowing in action that is valuable when anticipating difficulties, and preparing for new challenges. This can be effective in situations of conflict or uncertainty, when people with different perspectives can actually experience others' viewpoints, and in doing so, see their own position in a new way. By rehearsing options and reflecting on the bigger picture, decisions can be reached that are founded on a greater wisdom, than might otherwise have been available.

Walking Round the Tree

Another method that aids reflexive learning is to 'walk around the tree'. Whatever currently occupies my attention – a project, a person, a problem, a situation – I envisage as a tree. By walking round it and viewing it from unusual angles – maybe even climbing up into the branches – or hovering over it from above – or walking round to the back – it is possible for me to see many more perspectives than the one I am usually locked into. I can get a sense of myself and what I am doing and with luck can start to see the whole situation differently. This enables me to develop a 'third position'. Instead of getting stuck in my view, or a view that I am allied to, I am able to see both the others' perspective and a sense of the whole, which is neither me nor her – but both and what is happening between us. Conflict and difficulties between people are never far away and it is good to reflect on different perspectives and help others do the same – rather than simply take sides and reinforce the splits.

Turning Towards

When difficulties occur within groups of people – as they inevitably will – it is tempting to ignore them, in the hope that they will go away! But in the practice of development, which is explicitly focused on learning, difficulties can be useful. They stir the pot – so to speak – and offer opportunity to explore areas that are usually avoided, which invariably contain rich emotion and the possibility of qualitative change.

Turning towards the difficulty, and encouraging a process that opens to include it, is a sound practice that can reap significant rewards. It may not be possible to see where things are heading. Our role as practitioners is not to try to predict or manipulate the future, but just to be open to holding the space, remembering that the cultural conserve (or *status quo*) needs to be heard and expressed – and that resistance to change is not always negative or necessarily unwise. It takes time to integrate new learning, and for solutions to evolve that express both the energy that wants the change and the resistance that opposes it. Both energies are vital for healthy change.

Developing the Practitioner

As practitioners we need to practice on ourselves too, if we want to be in tune with others as they learn about themselves. It is really only possible to facilitate a learning process in others, if you yourself have experienced some insights out of your own process, and are open to learning more. This is a huge challenge for practitioners, who are already busy and stretched, and lack the time and energy. It is easier by far to have answers for others than be co-explorers in uncertainty. But how can we expect to support and enable others to develop, if we are not doing it ourselves.

There are no standardised requirements for an ongoing process of personal development. There are many ways to approach this, books galore, and methods abound that appeal differently to different people. We all have our own individual learning styles and preferences. The method is up to you. The intention to invest in ourselves is what counts. Personal learning can be practised anywhere and everywhere. We do not lack opportunity! The most useful quality for us to cultivate is probably one of openness to seeing things differently and letting go of old patterns. Life itself is the richest source of learning – reflecting us back to ourselves all the time.

5 Aligning with Intention – Working with Congruence

'You do not have to be good
You do not have to walk on your knees
For a hundred miles through the desert, repenting.
You only have to let the soft animal of your body
love what it loves'[6]

It is worth exploring why we do our work and discover what motivates us. In looking at this, many of us discover early experiences or influences that have affected us strongly. We can trace a path that started when we were quite young, that has taken us to who we are now. It is important to evaluate these influences and determine the ways in which they have developed us. We can learn a lot about ourselves through this process.

Intention is a mixture of values, beliefs, and commitment. It is another area of our lives that does not belong solely to the intellectual. It involves heart and emotions – passion and spirit even – and is a powerful driving force for the way we live our lives and we determine our priorities.

'The path to hell is paved with good intentions' – an old adage – but good intentions, offered lightly, are not what I refer to here. They are a distant cousin to this stronger, firmer conviction that comes from the guts and the heart of what really matters to us. Our intention is a commitment that when 'spoken' from the heart, brings tremendous power for good.

Working in ways that are aligned to our intention to benefit others is quite simply the best support to our practice that there is. It involves a process that goes way beyond the small considerations of personal success or failure. Of course, if the intention is self-seeking and materialistic, then the actions aligned to it will not benefit anyone but the actor. But, if the intention is to support people's intrinsic dignity, power and capacity to develop, then deliberately aligning to this will support us to do it.

Working with the Basic Good Qualities of People

Development work can involve us in the crucial business of enabling and supporting people in their full humanity – with all that involves. At best, the development process gives an opportunity to people (whether practitioners or local people) to realise and express their creativity, their values, and their intrinsic 'being' – the essence of who they are, if you like – never mind where they come from, what education they have had, or how they function in the world. This essence is the basis of the goodness of people and is in many ways, very simple and ordinary.

Would that there were more world leaders who exhibited these 'ordinary' good qualities and worked with awareness and confidence of them in others! The Dalai Lama is seen by some as a rare exception. He appears to show no hatred towards those who hurt him or his country people. Nelson Mandela is another such being, who seems to be able to touch others with compassion, commitment and ordinariness and yet still want things a certain way. They both have an ability to connect with others in an open, direct way – person to person, with warmth, simple humour and kindness. They illustrate ideas of 'personhood' or 'being' that highlights personal integrity, kindness and humility, often putting their own needs secondary to others.

It seems important to be able to recognise occasions when the intrinsic goodness of people shines through. However rare these times sometimes feel, it is then that love, creativity, and dignity are most evident.

In some ways, basic human goodness is very simple and ordinary, and is often easier to recognise in people who live relatively unsophisticated lives. Yet it exists naturally in us all – but like much else is often hidden.

Not So Much Building Capacity as Dismantling the Barriers

Development is often seen as a process that improves people in some way. Communities are said to have been developed when they are thought to be better than they were before. Within this view, it is as if disadvantaged people, who are thought to need developing, are similar to empty or half-empty vessels, which are filled up by a process that is called development, facilitated by a practitioner. People have the potential but their capacity must be 'built up', it is said, in order that they can function as well as possible as leaders, individuals, community or project members, and so on.

This view of a person and her development is widely held, but not accurate or helpful, I believe. Instead of needing to realise potential, people already possess their full capacity, which like the qualities of basic goodness, is already fully developed. The intrinsic qualities of 'personhood', which include creativity, natural kindness and wisdom, altruism, spontaneity, and full awareness exist perfectly already.

However there are multiple barriers and obstacles that get in the way of a complete expression of who we are. The metaphor often used to illustrate this, is the image of a jewel, already perfect in every way, but buried in dirt, so that only occasional glimpses of the facets shine through. The obstacles and the dirt are the causes and conditions that relate to how we live, think, behave and view the reality of our lives.

The special moments of gold that I mentioned in the previous chapter, are powerful times of connection, when conditions allow people to relate from the core of who they are and shine with the radiance of their interconnection, energy, well being, wisdom and goodness.

Walking The Talk

Working with congruence is the same as being aligned to intention. It relates to the way we translate our values into what we actually do, and how we behave with people. To genuinely and consistently 'walk our talk' is immensely challenging.

It is the pivotal point that shows us how genuine we are about our own personal learning and development. Without awareness, we cannot know whether our values are truly underpinning our practice – since it is less about the results that flow from our actions, and more about the intention that lies behind them.

Deliberately linking into the practice of being grounded in my experience offers a way of checking my personal congruence. Does this situation feel right? Am I comfortable when I do that? How do I feel when I say that? Our bodies will inform us, if we are aware, of the moment we act in ways that are untrue. There will be the sensation of a jolt or a lurch or a flutter that tells us that we have not acted genuinely – that the exchange was not 'clean'. Our bodies are wonderful lie detectors, if we are open to listening to them.

This is also important in monitoring our power as development practitioners. It is vital to find ways of reflecting on this in relation to our values and intention. This involves 'handing over the pen' whenever we can; checking our own need to succeed and get results; and reflecting on who owns the success – or how we explain failure to ourselves and others. Who gets the blame?

Integrity is so easily compromised in the interests of glory or success or in the projected interpretation of the moment. It is only our awareness that gives it to us straight and tells us how we are doing – if we are prepared to listen. Without it, we are inevitably lost in a sea of self-deception.

Maintaining the Vehicle

Many development practitioners go through periods of heavy work pressure. For some of us, this is an ongoing pattern. We promise ourselves that we will change after our next holiday, at the start of next year, when we change our job, sometime, never. Consistently overworking to a point of exhaustion is not conducive to congruent practice. It is literally impossible to be effective if we are drained, driven and near burn-out. It may appear right to prioritise the (much greater) needs of others, but it does not work. If we work in unhealthy ways, we are investing in an unhealthy system.

'Maintaining the vehicle' of our own well-being is essential, if we are to continue to work with integrity and stay well. It is only through congruent practice that we can effectively support others to grow, learn, be more powerful and creative in their lives, be well and happy. This involves us in ensuring we rest, relax, take time off, have a life outside work, eat regularly, have fun, see friends, and so on.

Deepak Chopra[7] reminds us that there are three forces pervading all life: creation, maintenance and destruction. It is up to us which aspect is dominant.

Those who choose creation tend to share certain traits, he suggests:

1. They are able to experience and enjoy silence

2. They spend time in nature

3. They trust their feelings

4. They remain centred amidst chaos

5. They are childlike – they enjoy play

6. They self refer: by continuing to explore and be curious

7. They are not rigidly attached to any one point of view: they remain open to new possibilities.

We also have a responsibility to support our practice through supervision, mentoring, peer support, counselling – whatever is appropriate and possible. We need skilful guidance if we are to remain open, reflexive, effective – and working at our creative 'edges'. Others, outside the loop, can reflect back and help us see the hidden areas that we might never spot on our own. We are wise if we choose people who have qualities we respect and who have established personal roles that wish to develop in ourselves.

Resonating Values and Intention

Our intention and personal values form the core of our practice, which radiate out, affecting every other aspect of how we work – influencing all our interactions, behaviours, and learning. As we come into contact with other people and networks – their practice and values resonate and influence us. As processes build and interventions develop, resonance or dissonance can expand or contract as values and principles coalesce or diverge. It is a simple and powerful system that constantly exchanges energy within itself and with others that connect to it.

If there is dissonance, conflict and difficulty will permeate the whole system. If there is a genuine alignment, there is the potential for connection and resonance, to bring powerful personal learning and opportunities for change and growth, affecting every person and every aspect of the interconnection.

This is at the heart, mind and guts of development practice – to work with the resonance and the dissonance, the creative and the difficult, the possible and the overwhelming – with integrity, heart, presence and learning.

And when the boundaries shift, everything changes again…

> 'Wisdom demands a new orientation of science and technology towards the organic, the gentle, the non violent, the elegant, the beautiful. Peace, as has often been said, is indivisible…But what is wisdom? Where can it be found?…It can be read about in numerous publications but it can be found only inside oneself.'[8]

Mamadile Terdla Mohuba

My name is Mamadile Terdla Mohuba. I live in Mashabela village and I am a primary school teacher teaching Maths, Sapedi, History, English and Geography to grades 4-7. This means I teach children aged 9 and upwards.

I have three children – two girls, aged five and 12, and a boy aged eight. My husband lives in Pretoria. He works as a technical assistant in the Transvaal museum and only comes home at the end of the month. We have lived like that ever since we were first married.

In 1997, when Manyaku was here in this village, I was a member of the Development Learning Group and one of the facilitators and leaders of the Women's Conference. I am also the secretary of the village electricity committee.

Women are involved in everything — it is just that they are shy to talk, especially in front of men. It doesn't mean that they lack something or they don't know. They are just shy. If you have a group of men and women, the men will dominate and the women will be quiet.

I have changed now — especially at school. I always want to talk. I don't want to listen any more and keep quiet. After attending all the development workshops in 1997, I became much more active. I have confidence now. In the past in meetings I would think inside myself, that I am going to say something wrong. Now I just say it, even if it is wrong or right! In the end I find it helps just to say what I think.

I empower my friend at school. She is always shy to talk. When she is asked questions in meetings, she doesn't speak. I tell her 'You must try to talk'. After the meeting she always tells me about her feelings. I tell her that if you don't talk, they may take a decision that you don't like, thinking that they have covered all of us. This helps her. She is talking a little bit now

At home, I'm always asking my husband to share things — like helping to prepare food for the children. Sometimes he does this — but then he says I am not respecting him.

I felt empowered by the women's conference. We organised it together — just we women. On the day, many women came and I was so happy that it was us, who had organised the whole day. We even funded it ourselves.

I even felt happy when I spoke at the conference. People listened to me and showed that they understood. There was lots of dancing and singing. We gave out trees and they are now bearing fruit. One woman told me that she so much enjoyed being only women and no men. It was our day.

In 1994, during the time of the first elections, the village was really united. People were attending workshops to be shown how to vote. On the day, I can say that 90% of the villagers came to the voting stations. I was one of the officials. We were running the election in most of the schools in the village. We started at about six am and everyone had finished by about two in the afternoon. It was wonderful!

When we do things jointly, it is easy to develop. If we meet and try to share ideas on how to bring electricity into our homes — then, when the villagers agree, it is then easy to send one person to enquire from ESKOM for all of us. It saves people going up and down (in taxis to Pietersburg) using their own money and getting nowhere.

If we work jointly, we always succeed. Development will fail if people don't understand, don't listen or stay away and look for one person to do everything.

I enjoyed being interviewed by Manyaku, the first time. We had just started working together in the Learning Group and there were some things that I couldn't say in front of the others. They were confidential things. After the interviews, when we were together, we knew each other more than before.

You cannot work with people if you don't love them – you will always be alone or with your children. If I didn't love Manyaku, I wouldn't agree to come and be interviewed. I would say I cannot go. If you love people – you listen and share ideas with them. That is what showing love means.

My message to people about development:

'*In development, working together and co-operating in groups is very necessary. It leads people to succeed. For me it is the most important thing to understand'.*

 FIVE

Conclusion

I love the dark hours of my being.
My mind deepens into them.
There I can find, as in old letters,
the days of my life, already lived,
and held like a legend, and understood.
Then the knowing comes: I can open
To another life that's wide and timeless.

Rainer Maria Rilke[1]

In this era of instant gratification, we want quick results. It is very human to look for definitive outcomes that shut down the opportunity to reflect more deeply; to look at an overall situation and judge it simply as good or bad. So often, we surf experience, only noticing the top of the crest or the bottom of the trough of the wave, and rarely appreciating the tiny gains or small little changes. We constantly return to look for single solutions and enduring truths that will resolve something forever – but they are not to be found. And sometimes this is heartbreaking.

The changing of individual experience cannot be delivered by others. This requires an internal and very personal awareness to shift – out of which new meanings can be found and shared with others like you. It is only out of this shift of understanding that change in behaviour and different opportunity is fully possible.

In Mashabela, questions remain about whether the personal experience of local people, as a result of the intervention, produced learning and development that endured and improved the quality of their lives. Did local Mashabela people get more power and control over the decisions and resources that affect their lives? This is perhaps the ultimate test for every development intervention.

We can point to the establishment of a village representative on the TLC (local authority funding body) and the appointment of a local woman to take this position. We can look at the increased maturity and confidence of the women leaders, who now take a more active, independent role in the women's projects, and to some extent in the village as a whole (school governors, village sub committees etc.). We can see that women are more confident in village matters, and their increased participation is experienced by the men. Young people have taken on a central role and a large part in running HIV/AIDS awareness programmes – and Maololo is more included in village decision-making, alongside some other outlying sub villages. Electricity and water have arrived for the majority of people living in the central communities of the village, and local people were involved with consultants as this was developed. The sanitation project finished its work, and other projects have come and gone.

These are the fairly obvious 'hard-ish' outcomes, which you could argue to some extent were linked to the work of the intervention. There are probably other less direct results, which could also be described. But do they show that as a result of the intervention, local people have increased power and control over the decisions and resources that affect their lives? I could argue that they do not – and certainly feel that it is not enough. Women are still exploited and marginalised, village education on the whole is pretty poor, Maololo does not have safe drinking water, poverty is widespread and most important of all, village people are dying of AIDS and children are being left as orphans.

At the same time I can make a good case for describing things in such a way that the evaluation is seen as positive. This would not be dishonest, but with a positive spin and in the context of the needs and activity of the area – the intervention, over the time involved, achieved some interesting outcomes.

At the end of the day, how *do* we judge our interventions? In most instances, how can we be sure that our work has offered enough benefit? How can we begin to assess whether we have used our craft with sufficient skill and congruence or not?

I have written about the way, as practitioner, I have to focus. I have no prescription for practice. Explore 'don't know' is probably the best I can suggest. But this, as I have tried to explain, is perhaps the finest and rarest practice of all, combining qualities of openness, respect, wisdom, courage, confidence and curiosity – and few of us can honestly claim these, even on a good day.

My primary intention in writing this book is to honour the Mashabela people and enable their presence to shine through, with the clarity of their message. I have sought to bring relationships centre stage in development, showing that connection and connecting are the basis of developing trust. I have highlighted the importance of the practitioner's own awareness as her primary development tool, which she needs to hone and sharpen with diligence. I have written about development practice that relates to people as already whole, which seeks to support them to realise their creativity, power and essential dignity – rather than see them as unfortunate victims, who need building up or improving in some way. Our own learning as practitioners is crucial to a process that has a chance of being genuinely rich for local people – and there is truth in the adage that we do the work with others that we most need to do on ourselves.

This book has sought to share the learning that came out of the development in Mashabela, in a way that is accessible and provokes development workers and others to reflect on their practice, whatever context they hail from. The questions that emerged from the process – and the issues contained in the learning – are relevant to development work wherever it is.

Love, Power and Learning were the overarching qualities that I used to frame my research and support my practice.

They speak to me still – and point to a path best navigated with the compass of reflective questioning – the course of genuine intention – the heart and mind of kind attention – and the footsteps of patience and trust in the face of uncertainty.

And the wind of change is always present as your friend or your foe.

'The breeze at dawn has secrets to tell you
Don't go back to sleep.
You must ask for what you really want.
Don't go back to sleep.
People are going back and forth across the doorsill
Where the two worlds touch.
The door is round and open.
Don't go back to sleep.'

Rumi[2]

Molefe Sello

My name is Molefe Mavis Sello. I am 28 years old and I have a baby girl of 18 months old. I live in Mashabela, a village in South Africa.

I qualified as a teacher at Sekgosese College, near Tzaneen, in Limpopo, in 1995, but I have only had temporary teaching posts since then and have otherwise been unemployed. I live with my mother and my child.

In 1997, when Manyaku was here, I was in the Learning Group and was secretary of the Mashabela village water committee. I was also a member of the facilitators and census teams and spoke on behalf of the youth at the Women's Conference.

In the past, we were afraid of being with people who were different to us (white people). We never met people from outside or shared our ideas with them. But now, we have learned that we are equal – and in our equality, we can share what we have.

After the workshops, I felt that I can do something for my community.

In the beginning I was unable to speak. I was having a fear of the unknown. I did not know what I feared, but I was very frightened. I was attending workshops with my teachers and people older than me. But as time went on, I discovered that sharing ideas can be good and you can understand many things that you didn't understand before. People think that my ideas are good. Sometimes at a meeting when other people come with an idea that I disagree with, I put up my hand and say, 'No, I disagree with you'. In the beginning I was afraid to say 'no' but now I am active. Yes!

We have learnt that the people living in the village are the experts. The Mashabela people are the experts. We know what we need and what needs to be done.

We come together and ask the people and they say we need this and this. Then from the list, we can chose the first priority – the community can choose themselves. Everyone takes part in saying what she needs and then we can group the answers and ask them what is the most important. I am working on the water committee, which is always the most important need.

I have learnt that knowledge not only comes from school. Learning is everywhere. I have learnt a lot from my child. Her mind is full of new things. You can say that the child does not know. But she knows a lot that you didn't know. Learning starts from home. If you teach with love, your children will always be interested in your lesson. And they'll feel good.

When I have problems, I just remember them all the time and then I question whether I am failing and the learning becomes difficult.

In the Learning Group, I enjoyed facilitating meetings and giving speeches when there were visitors. I was quite exposed but I liked being together and sharing ideas especially with the women. I feel much more confident now. In days ago, women didn't express themselves, but now we are able to.

I came late to the women's conference from a funeral. There were many many women there and they were all very happy and active. I arrived just in time to be called to give a speech about youth. I was unprepared but it was ok. The conference was very well organised and went as it was planned. Terdla, Julia, Altah and some others organised it and we women funded it ourselves. After the conference we were given some trees, but mine was eaten by the goats!

At all our village meetings the sub village is now represented. When we make a decision we can let all the people know through their representatives. The sub village process influenced this.

Our village is now better known because we have a TLC member from Mashabela. We have the new clinic, which is electrified. The gardens have improved – we are now planting according to the right methods. We have got workshops from outside. Education has improved and attendance is better. The children are even coming to the winter school and the Saturday schools.

I am happy with the way Mashabela is developing. The work that we did in 1997 is guiding us. We know where we are going. We have a plan.

My message to people about development:

'The community can do development on their own. When consultants come from outside, they must also consult the community to find the way.'

Six

The Development Context
in South Africa and in the UK

*These two essays by Loretta van Schalkwyk and David Robinson describe the
context for development in both South Africa and Britain and outline some of
the key challenges, constraints, developments, and debates currently taking
place.*

*Significant elections were held in the 1990s, which to different degrees
changed the face of development in both countries.*

*In South Africa, the first democratic elections, held in 1994, were a landmark
in the history of the country. The effect on the development sector, and the rapid
social change that swept through the country, is still being played out.* **Loretta
van Schalkwyk** *writes about this in the first section of this chapter. She has been
keenly involved in supporting change in South Africa all her life. She is based in
Durban, supporting the learning and development of people and organisations
in the development sector.*

The South African Context by Loretta van Schalkwyk

I asked a political leader from Sekhukhuneland what a white woman
community worker from Britain could bring to a remote and very poor rural
village in the province of South Africa known as Limpopo. 'She brings hope,'
he replied, 'and more importantly, she brings recognition to the people that to
someone, somewhere, they are important. She also brings a window to
something else being possible for the people in the village where she is working'.

The themes of presence, hope, recognition and affirmation will emerge later
in this introduction.

First let us examine the context.

The Apartheid Years

At the height of Apartheid in the mid-1950s to early 1970s, South Africa was systematically divided into ethnic 'homelands'. Hundreds of thousands of black people were 'relocated' (often forcibly) to bare-earth rural areas. There, with arrogant supremacy, the government of the day declared that 'they would be enabled to develop along their own lines in their own time'. Apartheid – separate development – was rapidly institutionalised, controlling and creeping into every sphere of black people's lives.

The relocation of people to rural areas brought conflict between black and black. People traditionally established in or around the relocation areas frequently resented the newcomers who would now be competing for already scarce resources.

Among many other assumptions, Apartheid appeared to assume that all black people were rural and agrarian by nature. However, many of those who were relocated had never lived outside of an urban area – they brought with them urban aspirations and a certain urban sophistication. They had little or no knowledge about subsistence farming or animal husbandry. They also brought a challenge to the rural traditional customs and accepted ways of life.

The more orderly traditional 'umuzis' or homesteads were starkly contrasted with the shacks built of corrugated iron, the fragile board and plastic bag structures and the 'outside' bucket or 'long drop' lavatories that started dotting the landscape. The veldt was quickly denuded of any trees as they were used either as frame poles for the houses or to provide firewood for cooking. The interior walls of the makeshift houses were lined with newspaper as insulation against heat and cold.

Rain was both blessing and curse. There were no taps or running water – with luck there was a river. Rain filled the rivers and washed away the pollution of overcrowding. Rain irrigated the struggling gardens and maize fields. Rain leaked into the houses and turned the spaces between them into muddy quagmires. Rain fell too much, and the crops were drowned. Rain fell too seldom and too little, and people went hungry.

White farmers were favoured. Dams were built to secure electoral votes. Rivers that had previously fed many of the areas dried up or became a mere trickle. Overcrowding reduced the trickle to sand. Flood plains were destroyed and traditional farming methods could no longer succeed.

Through relocation and overcrowding, cattle and goats that had always represented a person's status, wealth, and well-being increased beyond the capacity of the land. Overgrazing became a problem.

A pattern of enforced environmental degradation was established among people who previously had nurtured the land and valued its trees and plants as food, medicine, shelter, and grazing.

Political oppression and a wide combination of other social and economic factors built a deep resentment between groups – white against white, white and black against white, black against white and black against black. Black leaders who accepted the homeland status of their newly defined areas were seen by progressive groups as 'sell-outs' supporting the principles of Apartheid. Those who refused recognition or who held out against it for as long as possible were caught in an impossible dilemma. Refuse, and then get no financial and other support from the government at the cost of the people. Accept, and be scorned.

All this, in one way or the other, fed a deeper and bitter hatred of the Apartheid government and created divisions between groups. Many of these continue to the present day. Trust was broken down and the divide and rule policies of the day led to understandably extreme paranoia. Families were pitted against one another through differing political allegiances or through 'counter-insurgency' planted lies. Relationships were reduced to a minimum. The less you knew, the less likely you could be forced to reveal information about another under the oppressive policing of the Apartheid regime.

Young people were quickly recruited into solidarity with the Africa National Congress (ANC – the present government) or the Pan-African Congress (PAC). Both these groups were banned, along with the South African Communist Party and moved into underground activity.

Civil Society Under Apartheid

Under the draconian legislation of Apartheid, it was not easy for civil society organisations to form or to function. Where organisations did emerge, these were closely monitored by the security police. Materials were confiscated and people working in the organisations were frequently taken in for questioning, held in detention and banned. It was difficult to get funding into the country and money had to be brought in surreptiously. In an attempt to monitor both the flow of money and the activities of the organisation, the government introduced legislation which required any 'development', welfare, or service organisation to register if it were to be allowed to receive funds from overseas.

In the early 1970s, Black Consciousness leader, the late Steve Biko and his followers established a system of community-based resource centres to bring denied resources to people at a grass roots level. They were barely established and running, when these were closed down by the police and all the materials confiscated. Steve Biko, a most extraordinary and inspired young leader, died at the hands of the security police as did many other black and white activists working towards a better and more equitable society.

Also at this time pressure began to mount from an emergent trade union movement. The ANC's official trade union movement (SACTU) had been banned. A strong and progressive trade union movement, the Federation of South African Trade Unions, (FOSATU) became a force to be reckoned with, taking up the cause of black workers who were unable to belong to trade unions and could only be represented through so called Coloured or Indian unions. Although banning orders were slapped on a number of the intellectuals and worker leaders interacting with FOSATU, the grouping strategically pressurised companies through the powerful tool available to trade unions with a threat to withhold labour if recognition agreements were not signed; and through the publicising of inequities in companies with overseas shareholders. Although striking was illegal, a precedent of forceful strikes had been set in Durban and in Cape Town in the early 1970s.

FOSATU subsequently developed into the Congress of South African Trade Unions, COSATU. These organisations played a significant role in the growing awareness of political and class issues of workers and, ironically, also in a number of cases, the 'bosses' of the factories where they worked. The trade union pressure was for the overthrow of apartheid (social and political equality) and the redistribution of wealth (economic equality). The thinking was strongly Marxist influenced.

In the case of many of the other anti-apartheid organisations, both liberal and more radical, the focus was purely to rid South Africa of apartheid on the assumption that other inequities would then be automatically corrected.

Certain of the churches were instrumental in starting and supporting organisations which emerged to contest and fight apartheid. Notable in this regard was the work of the South African Council of Churches; the Diakonia Ecumenical Centre in Natal; Black Sash (an organisation of liberal white woman who engaged in public protest wearing black sashes and were subject to frequent police harassment); the various Advice Centres established by the Black Sash and separately, by progressive lawyers; human rights bodies; civic organisations (in the mid 1980s to late 1990s); an educational group, SACHED; housing associations; student bodies such as Congress of South African Students (COSAS) – a black student movement – and the National Union of Students of South Africa (NUSAS) on white campuses, and many other groupings.

Also of significance was the Afrikaanse Sendingskerk – a break-away group from the established churches that supported the Nationalist government. Working primarily in the rural areas with a large number of black and so-called coloured members, the 'kerk' assisted in the formation of community groups and in putting pressure on the government to urgently change.

A highly significant movement was the United Democratic Front which brought together numerous anti-apartheid organisations and, acting as a front for the exiled ANC, mobilised pressure against the government at schools, tertiary institutions, in black townships and in the cities. Black and white were drawn together around the common cause of 'apartheid must go'. Ironically some of the organisations which joined the movement were not even or only vaguely aware of the ANC connection.

Populist uprisings in the black areas, worker pressure, South Africa's military might losing ground in the war in Angola, pressure from business and churches, overseas sanctions and pressures led to the commencement of discussions with the ANC in exile. This subsequently culminated in the release of Nelson Mandela after 25 years of prison and the beginning of negotiations for a shift in the power relations in South Africa.

At the time, most of the civil society organisations were known as 'community-based' and the term Non Government Organisation (NGO) was generally reserved to refer to Northern NGOs. Some were operating formally, others were a collection of concerned citizens who organised nationally, around campaigns such as the Free Mandela campaign and Prisoners' Rights campaign. Psychologists and counsellors volunteered time to work with released and traumatised detainees.

Money for organisation was channelled by the northern NGOs directly to the organisations or through intermediary groups and because of the climate of the time, in most cases; little accountability and real relationship was required from the recipient organisations. At the time, and in the main, it was sufficient that the South African groups were working towards the overthrow of apartheid. It was a relationship of trust. The local organisations were highly dependent on the money from overseas. This dependence exacerbated the imbalance of the power relationship between north and south.

In the longer term (by the late 1980s early 1990s) all this was to have challenging consequences for established and emerging NGOs in South Africa. Up until this time, the northern donors, in their opposition to the apartheid regime, had not entered into bilateral agreements with the government of the day. As South Africa moved towards change, the northern donors began signalling that in the future they would have to limit funding directly to NGOs and CBOs and that money would need to be accessed through the bilateral agreements that they would be entering once a democratic government was in place in South Africa.

South African NGOs and CBOs were forced to begin to redefine their relationships with the Northern donors. They found themselves pressured to rapidly learn how to draw acceptable budgets and to be rigidly accountable for the money. The new requirements shifted the more loosely organised groupings into more bureaucratic structures with more clearly defined Vision, Purpose and Indicators of success. More professionalism and 'management' skills were demanded.

In many instances, this succeeded in moving many NGOs further away from direct contact with people on the ground and putting them into a role of servicing the organisations which ostensibly were in direct contact with community-based organisations and the people on the ground.

Political education and the direct building of relationships with the people on the ground quickly dwindled in the push for efficiency and effectiveness of organisational operation. There was a scramble for donor money to build organisations rather than to organise.

Donors strongly influenced local organisations' 'purpose' in how they allocated money: for instance ABET (everyone was suddenly doing literacy); leadership training (everyone was engaged in leadership training); gender, HIV/AIDS, etc. All these were necessary and good causes, but led more by what some northern donors saw to be important, rather than the more specific real needs and priorities of different groups of people in different areas.

Within the organisations, people began challenging one another to be clearer about their political affiliation and 'comradeship' – ANC, PAC, social democratic, communist, and liberal. Power relations were challenged and in some cases this led to polarisation between white and black staff.

In some cases, NGOs and CBOs were 'high jacked' by political groupings or indulged in their own internal navel gazing at the cost of engagement with their 'client' groups. Relationship-building both internally and externally slid down the ladder of priorities.

Debate on the role of NGOs/CBOs as organs of civil society was minimal. For many, a sense was expressed that once 'our' government is in place, there will surely no longer be a need for NGOs/CBOs.

The confusion and turbulence in the ranks was understandable given the boiling point pressure of the times and the really passionate need for the 1994 elections to bring real democracy to South Africa and an end to apartheid.

The situation was not all bleak. While some significant NGOs/CBOs fell by the wayside of change, many were strengthened and new and exciting formations began to emerge. Some were engaged in closely examining the social movements of central and South America. They began to explore, debate and consider the possibilities of civil society and its important role of challenge to ensure just and strong government. This was done with an awareness that challenge from civil society against a newly formed democratic government might well be seen as disloyalty.

This has proved true.

Notwithstanding, at the time of writing some very powerful organisations and movements have or are emerging around land, environmental and most particular HIV/AIDS issues. Civil society in South Africa is slowly but forcefully beginning to sharpen its teeth in taking up issues of social, economic and political importance. Apartheid as it was known might be dead, but apartheid issues have not disappeared.

While for many years, most of the NGO activity functioned out of urban or border urban areas, with field workers moving into rural areas, the situation is changing.

NGOs and CBOs are being directly challenged by the concept that effective organisation is about building relationships within the organisation, between organisations, and most importantly with the client base.

The words 'relationships', 'networking' and 'partnership' for development have strong currency. They are in danger of becoming mere rhetoric. There are many who challenge their meaning.

The Promise of Change

In the late 1980s and early 1990s change began to come to South Africa. This culminated in 1994 with the country's first democratic elections. The present ANC government was voted into power under the leadership of Nelson Mandela – a South African and international icon. With the elections, transformation seemed instant – most people were euphoric. What many did not realise at first was the fact that to make the transformation real would take many years of negotiated transition. Transformation was relatively easy. Transition is about negotiating and fighting for legitimate meaning of transformation in social, economic and political terms. The battle is waged between rightwing, liberal, leftwing, and ultra left each feeling that theirs is the most legitimate definition. Indeed, during the time the author of this book was working in Limpopo and (up to the present day) South Africa continues to work on and through transition. It is still moving, slowly, and sometimes painfully, towards the goal of a democratic and enlightened society in which all citizens have the right and the means to live in dignity as guaranteed by our Constitution.

This means that, while many things have changed, much has not changed or is still changing. Caught in the Catch-22 of apartheid backwash and costs, globalisation, tradition and modernity and the rapid pace of modern change, South Africa continues to follow a neo-liberal economic policy which benefits the rich and the corporate sector and makes little difference to, or even further impoverishes, the lives of the poor.

The state still lacks the capacity to provide basic services and infrastructure to all – particularly in rural areas. Unemployment remains extremely high – in the region of 35-40% (depending on which statistics are used), and HIV/AIDS is an almost overwhelming pandemic and threat. In some areas the incidence of HIV/AIDS is up to 35%. In many villages and towns, every weekend is given to funerals, and the number of orphans (both infected and non-infected) is rising all the time substantially. At the same time, the government has not taken a firm position on the epidemic.

I will now turn to the context of Sekhukhuneland, where the story around which this book is built occurred.

Sekhukhuneland: Tensions and Contradictions

Sekhukhuneland is an area in which a mixture of settled and relocated people live. It is a place with a powerful history of strong leadership in both a traditional and an informal context, and a long history of defiance against colonialism and later, against the structures of apartheid.

A mission hospital in the area has played a significant role in bringing modern medicine and health care to the area and in the apartheid era it also played an important role as a political haven and as a place of 'political discussion'.

Under the Apartheid laws, separate education, 'Bantu' education, was introduced into black schools. Mission schools that were not prepared to change to the system, had their subsidies cut and many were forced to close. Mission stations, despite elements of patronisation, played an important role in providing library and other resources denied to the average black child in a rural area. Private schools, although elitist, also played an important role in this connection.

Various NGOs and CBOs have also played a significant role in the area on issues of housing, land, environmental justice, health and claims against mines for victims of asbestosis, training and development. One NGO has established a community radio station.

But villages are widely dispersed. Unemployment is rife. Many men move to the cities in search of work. They do not always return or send remittances back to their families. Children are often cared for by grandparents and entirely dependent on the old age pension of R640 (currently) per month. With luck, and the correct documentation the grandparent might know that she/he is entitled to a childcare grant of R100 for each of the children under the age of 6 years. Plans are afoot to increase this grant and to extend the qualification to the age of 14 years.

Life is tough. Subsistence farming is dependent on the weather and drought is commonplace in the area. People with HIV need a diet high in fresh vegetables and fruit. This is not always affordable or available. Crops are unpredictable.

Traditional forms of authority are still strong and respected. In conversation with some people from the area recently, they spoke of the struggle to hold onto and value the traditional ways of living and leading, while at the same time moving into modernity. This is not always shared by young people, who are attracted by the bright lights of neighbouring cities where smart clothes and possessions get you street 'cred.' This very often means that young people, unable to find employment, turn to crime.

A real problem is the absence of authority role models who have managed to hold a balance between tradition and modernity; between old values and the demands of status of the 'new' world. The role models of the young, who gain respect and attention, tend to do so as a consequence of the position they hold coupled with flamboyant material success. Respect, success and purchasing power have become intimately linked.

In relation to HIV/AIDS there is an enormous feeling of helplessness in some communities. People have got the message that there is no cure. Funerals are commonplace – up to four every weekend. Awareness is slowly taking root. But the pandemic is far advanced, and collecting condoms from the nearest clinic is not high on the agenda when a daily water supply has to be collected two to five kilometres away. Nor is it high on the agenda of a woman whose husband returns home drunk, demanding sex, and threatening to beat her up if this is refused.

For many in rural areas, life is a constant struggle for survival…trying to feed hungry children; trying to find school fees and money for school uniforms; trying to grow meagre crops; to protect chickens from predators; to graze the odd goat or cow. Trying to find fire wood and to ensure a supply of enough water for washing, cooking, and drinking. A woman in rural areas works an average of fourteen hours a day.

Recognition and affirmation are rare. Yet amongst one another there is still loving and caring for children, for the healthy, for the sick and the dying, and for the elderly and the disabled.

What Hope is There?

Surprisingly, given this situation, there is quite a lot of hope and reason to be hopeful.

Despite the hardships and difficulties, many people are organising to bring about change; to improve their own lives and those of the people of their area. Even an enormous shadow on the scale of the HIV/AIDS epidemic contains glimmerings of light. In many communities vibrant and committed groups of people are engaging with, caring for and beginning to change attitudes around infected people and the disease itself. Such changes are easy to miss, but they are the foundations of real change. It is these initiatives and this energy that development practitioners need in order to support and help groups, organisations and social movements to build on. Any developmental engagement needs to build trust, hope, self-respect and the capacity for self-reliance – all qualities that are desperately needed, but in short supply.

Further cause for hope is the shift in the world to a greater consciousness of gender and of the need to promote and build gender equity. The lives of women in general (including rural women) have begun to change, as they are finding their voices and begin to question their lot. (Admittedly, this has begun to happen more with middle-class, educated women than with women who survive by subsistence farming.) Rural women do however, have greater confidence to begin to talk about sexual abuse and domestic violence; previously taboo subjects.

Part of the work of development is about redeveloping a sense of morality; a deep sense of ethics that has been eroded by Apartheid and by the inexplicable hardships of the years that followed (HIV/AIDS in particular). The role of organising and working at community level demands the activity of working with people, not for them. It demands listening to their stories and valuing their experiences. It means total empathy and working with them to engage in the process of making meaning and direction for their own lives. It means helping them to answer the questions that will enable them to begin to take control of their own lives.

What then is development?

In the context discussed above, it can be argued that development is change in the direction of people having the capacity to live their lives in dignity. This requires that the people (with others) are able to meet their basic needs for shelter, food, water, sanitation, and, just as importantly, their needs for meaning, for power, and for the freedom to love and to be loved.

Development can be said to have begun when there has been an enhancement of people's belief in their right to be in the world, and to ask challenging questions of those in power. Ultimately, the capacity to be and do in this way emerges from a sense that we have some control of our own lives. This sense of control – seeing oneself as being able to exercise leadership over one's own life, is attained through increasing own awareness and self-respect and a respectful awareness of others.

Facilitating development, then, is about creating opportunities for people to develop self-awareness, confidence, and the capacity to challenge the *status quo* in meaningful and strategic ways. It is also about supporting them in taking their first steps in exercising this new leadership in their own lives.

Development at Local Level:
Balancing the Individual and the Group

In my view, 'community' is not a very useful word. It is too loosely used. It implies 'happy families'. In fact it can mean anything from a grouping of two or three like-minded people working for a common purpose, to a whole conflict-ridden district of extreme diversity.

Therefore it is perhaps more useful to speak of 'the people of an area'. This avoids the implication of homogeneity in the word 'community'. Experience has shown that you start from the wrong premise if you begin by hoping to develop a 'community' particularly if it is on the assumption that 'community' is 'good' and the only way of achieving change or social movement. Rather, it is important to recognise that any group of people is made up of unique individuals, each with her own aspirations, interests, hang-ups, needs, mental models, and talents and abilities. The task of the development practitioner is to support them in finding ways to explore and expand their uniqueness while they are co-operating around some common purpose for the greater good. This also involves the identification and contracting of shared values and ethics Thus, it is the role of the practitioner to support both the individual and the group – effective results (and so, the potential for real change and development) occur when each person is enabled to contribute as fully as possible out of her creative imagination and individuality. Their capacity is then channelled and united in work towards an agreed purpose, founded on the agreed principles and ethics.

What is termed 'community development' is, at its best, about interacting with people to assist them to find ways to build understanding and co-operation between individuals and groups to enable them to make change in their own lives and for the greater good. Indeed, this is the foundation of most developmental practice, and is what this book is about.

What is a development practitioner?

A development practitioner is a person who has a deep sense of who they are, and strives for authenticity in how they position themselves respectfully in other people's lives. Their role is to enable the development and transformation of themselves, of others and of situations. They do this by listening deeply, questioning, challenging, and creating opportunities for people to see themselves and their realities in new ways. To do this requires a passionate belief that it is the birthright of all human beings to be whole people in this world. In other words, the foundation for a developmental practice is love of humanity in all its particular forms. I am privileged to write this introduction for a practitioner who strives towards, and often succeeds in, embodying this ideal.

As a true community worker, Trish Bartley moved into a rural village. She sought out people who held a leadership position in the village and others who were perceived to be leaders. She worked quietly in developing relationships and then offered people an opportunity to engage in a process designed to assist them in finding the questions that would enable them to begin to take more control of their own lives and to challenge the *status quo*. She engaged with them with respect, sometimes with naïvety, but always with a sense of love and the right of everyone in the village to have a place in holding up the sky.

Loretta van Schalkwyk
Durban, 2003

Marumo Cedric Makau

My name is Marumo Makau. I am 33 years old and have a young son. I hope to live with him and his mother one day soon.

I teach Biology, Agricultural Science and Sapedi at Ngonyeletse High School.

I live at Maololo village and was involved as a leader of the census team in 1997. I also used to be on the village Education Committee – because I am very concerned about the young people in this village, especially those who do not come to school.

I was very happy when I started working at this school in 1994. I had been under pressure and my mind was relieved to have got a job. I was also pleased because I wanted to help the children of this village. I think I started to be a little bit more responsible then!

In this school, they made me a treasurer and also the sports organiser. I suppose I empowered others by delegating tasks and by encouraging them too – especially the young people at school. People get more involved when they are empowered like that.

When there are problems, we work together well, if we can share ideas. For example in my village Maololo, which is a small village, this happened when we were busy trying to combat crime – and also when we built the schools for the children.

Love is the seed. When the people love each other, they are going to work well together. I feel happy when this happens, because it means there is a going to be a development result at the end. I love my village very much because we have beautiful mountains around us and the lay out of our land is beautiful. I love the way the people work together and because crime is not high. Then again I love my village, because I love farming. I most want to be a stock farmer.

Yes, I love the people in my village. Some do not love me very much but I love them all!

We have some problems in Maololo, like not having a proper water system.

We are not as involved in village affairs as we used to be, because of the river, which is flooded and hard to cross. It stops us from coming over – because we have no road or bridge.

In the workshops, I learnt about management and still remember how we managed the work in the census team. I started by getting people involved through sharing ideas. It is good to be open, and then everybody can ask whatever she or he wants.

Sometimes I think there are arguments and conflict in the village because of tribalism – or because of power. They are fighting for feuds. This is when we lose (ground in) development.

I think that the learning we did then (in 1997) still affects the village. For example at this side of the road, there is a project for farming – and at the side of Mashabela Primary School, there are some women's projects.

The women have changed. They are active now and can manage their own projects. Before 1997, they were not very active. They used to feel inferior. But now they do not. They are strong and run their own things.

But I am still worried about the young people. They are not involved. I am especially worried about those who have dropped out of school. I want to reach them to help them.

My message to people about development:

'Try to share your ideas because then you can succeed in whatever you are doing. I think that love is the most important seed that you need in development!'

The UK Context by David Robinson

*In the UK, the Labour Government was elected in 1997, after 18 years of Conservative governments, which were marked by cuts in public spending and a reduction in the role of local authorities. While this change is not as significant as the impact of the South African elections, nonetheless Tony Blair's government has tried to make changes in the way that local communities, especially those that are disadvantaged and excluded, are served and supported. **David Robinson**, Senior Advisor at **Community Links**, a leading community organisation in Newham, London, is well placed to comment on these changes and the effects that they have had on local development in the UK.*

Surveying the Scene

Years ago I remember a colleague telling me about an international conference on education, which drew together practitioners from across the world. In the first workshop she heard a teacher from the North talk at length about the software programmes that he had been developing for his students. The results were spectacular. The group turned their attention to the second speaker. 'We' she said, 'use sticks in the dirt. The results are spectacular'.

Suppose we combine the two: the sophisticated technology of a society that has wired the world and the highly developed personal skills of a community that can educate and inspire without any equipment at all. Now that would be spectacular.

A Sense of Belonging

Technological advances have revolutionised our relationships over a single generation here in the North. Community, travel, education have all been transformed. These are extraordinary developments but they have come at a price. As we have embraced a far wider network of relationships, many of us have lost the sense of belonging. We are no longer part of a community pursuing common interests, doing things together.

In 'Bowling Alone',[1] Professor Robert Putnam has recently shown how declining rates of participation in an identifiable community have damaged the health of the individual (mental illness), the health of the neighbourhood (crime rates) and the health of the wider society (voter turn out). On a different scale we have, through our practical work at Community Links, seen similar trends over the last 25 years and, especially amongst the young, increasingly serious disaffection.

As society has become more mobile, involvement in and dependence on the local community have become less important, but have not been replaced by a corresponding sense of belonging to or responsibility for a wider community. Relatively few people, for instance, join movements concerned with the global environmental issues which are such a huge threat to our children, if not to us. We shouldn't be nostalgic about outmoded structures, and trying to rebuild the urban communities which existed 50 years ago would be as unrealistic today as it would have been for our 19th Century ancestors to try to rebuild the rural communities which existed before the industrial revolution. We do need to find ways of establishing a *new* sense of belonging. Community development, here in the North, has never been more important.

Historical Background

Personal and community development take place in the context of the wider society, which in turn is shaped by history. British society began to take its present form in the mid-1970s, with a challenge to a consensus which had lasted 30 years. That consensus supported the 'welfare state' – a package including full employment; redistributive taxes; state ownership of the major utilities and some manufacturing industry; a national health service free at the point of use; rights for trade unions; public housing for rent; a broad remit for local government to provide care for vulnerable social groups; and a range of state benefits paid direct to individuals. However, despite decades of these policies, neither poverty nor inequality had been eliminated.

The challenge to this consensus was summed up in the term 'Thatcherism', named after the dominant figure of Margaret Thatcher, leader of the Conservative Party 1975-1990 and Prime Minister 1979-1990. But the Conservatives remained in power for another seven years with John Major as Prime Minister (1990-1997) and many 'Thatcherite' policies remained in force even after the Labour Party came into power in 1997 under the leadership of Tony Blair. The underlying idea, which goes back a lot further than Margaret Thatcher, is that money is better left in the hands of individuals than taken by the State, however the state spends it. There is an emphasis on individual self-reliance rather than reliance – or dependency – on the state. Margaret Thatcher famously believed that 'there is no such thing as society'.

Some of the policies associated with Thatcherism were: a willingness to tolerate high levels of unemployment; cuts in direct taxes, which effectively made the tax system less redistributive; the 'privatisation' of utilities and industries; legislation to weaken trade unions; the 'right to buy' for tenants of public housing; tight financial controls on local government; and real-terms cuts in benefits. The National Health Service and local authority schools remained in place, but were starved of funds.

The cumulative effect of these policies was to increase inequality and poverty. The rich grew richer – and that included the middle classes and working class people in good jobs – while unemployed people, those in low-paid jobs, and those who relied on pensions and benefits, either stayed poor or got poorer. A recent survey concluded that Britain is the most unequal country in the developed world after New Zealand, with a wealth gap between the richest and poorest in society wider than in Ethiopia or Ghana. Since 1979, the richest ten per cent of the British population have seen their income rise by 65% in real terms, whilst the income of the poorest ten per cent has actually dropped by 13%. When the Conservatives left office, one in three children lived below the poverty line – the highest rate of child poverty in the European Union.

Poverty and Inequality

Readers in some countries may be surprised to see the word 'poverty' used in discussing a rich country like the UK. Yet there is both absolute and relative poverty in this country. There are people sleeping in the streets, and beggars. There are neighbourhoods in the big cities and smaller towns which were heavily dependent on employment in failed industries, in which all the measures of well-being – employment, income, education, health, housing, freedom from crime – are significantly worse than the national average. The different aspects of poverty are cumulative and sometimes mutually self-perpetuating, often affecting several generations of the same family, and reinforced by prejudice and discrimination against disabled people, racial minorities, refugees, and asylum seekers. The result may be feelings of powerlessness, despair, and self-destructive nihilism, expressed in domestic violence, drug and alcohol abuse, truanting from school, vandalism, and crimes against other members of the poor community. This despair reduces the chances of individuals escaping from poverty, and gives encouragement to those in the prosperous majority who say that poor people have only themselves to blame. Individuals, families, and whole communities are marginalised and liable to fall further behind as mainstream society continues to become more prosperous. They are said to suffer 'social exclusion'.

Community Development

Well-known international development charities such as Oxfam and Save the Children work with poor people and communities in the UK, and there is a home-grown community development movement of which Community Links is a good example. I can begin to explain what I mean by the term 'community development' by describing our main areas of work

Community Links believes that we all have the potential to do great things. Our purpose is to tackle the causes and consequences of social exclusion by developing and running first-rate practical activities in East London and by sharing the local experience with practitioners and policy makers nationwide.

Community Links' work with young people in the London Borough of Newham, which has the youngest population in London and the highest level of youth unemployment, aims to encourage everyone to believe in their own potential. Over the last 25 years we have learnt that every child can succeed, though some are denied the opportunity. We aim high, support one another and get there together.

We have learnt that every adult can build their own ladder out of poverty or disadvantage. Some need advice, training or practical help and all reach further, faster together. We provide food and clothes, give advice on benefits and debt, run training courses, and offer the opportunity to participate, to share the experience, and to help others. Alone, these activities, and more, are limited in what they can achieve. Together, they are rungs on a ladder. Working in an area where one in three households has an income below £141 per week, and where half of the people who contact us are not in full receipt of their benefit entitlement, our involvement needs to be far-reaching and long-term.

It is important to share the lessons of building vibrant communities, both directly to other communities and to national decision-takers and policy-makers. Our advice and information to others is always soundly based on our experience in delivering first-rate practical services to the local community and pioneering new ideas.

Labour's First Term

The Labour Party came to power in 1997 and has subsequently been returned for a second term. During their first weeks in office the new administration launched the Social Exclusion Unit right at the heart of government. Within a year the Unit had published *Bringing Britain Together: A National Strategy for Neighbourhood Renewal* and established 18 Policy Action Teams. Their role was, in the words of Moira Wallace, the Unit's Director, 'fast track policy development on some of the most intractable problems facing communities living in deprived neighbourhoods across the country'.

The PAT process was a new approach to policy making. It brought together residents from deprived neighbourhoods, practitioners, professionals, academics, and civil servants. All the PATs had reported by April 2000 and, collectively, they made almost 600 recommendations. Their work formed the basis of the Action Plan published in January 2001 and ambitiously entitled *A New Commitment to Neighbourhood Renewal: National Strategy Action Plan*.

The *Action Plan*, and the process for producing it, was ambitious and without precedent, but they weren't the only initiatives in this field during Labour's first term. The £1.4 billion Sure Start programme will help 400,000 children under five, and their families, in 500 projects. The new Children's Fund and Local Network were launched with particular emphasis on small community groups and local neighbourhood work. The New Deal programme was to reduce unemployment throughout the country and both the Chancellor and the Prime Minister were personally identified with the visionary goal of eliminating child poverty within 20 years. By the start of Labour's second term, the number of children living in poor households had been reduced by close to one million. In the 2001 election campaign the Chancellor committed himself to lifting a second million out by 2005. In our most deprived communities these important changes will make huge differences in the lives of individual families.

After 18 years which were marked by cuts in public spending and a reduction in the role of local agencies, voluntary and statutory, there were whispered complaints about 'initiative-itis'. This was almost too much to handle, funds appeared to overlap, and for some organisations on the ground it was sometimes hard to identify a coherent strategy for connecting all this sudden activity. 'Joined-up government' was a buzz word for the first term but for many of us at the delivery end it often felt like anything but. However, there was movement. Effective communities were once again a concern of government and I, like many others, found that for the first time in my working life it was possible to bring to the minister's door the experience of the family at ours. There were and would be arguments about the content and the pace of development but the climate had changed.

Recent Developments

In 2001, the government was returned for a second term. The majority was even more decisive but the euphoria, ironically, more muted. Clearly there was a flurry of activity in the first term and all the right rhetoric, but what did it all add up to? For many people, the changes on the ground seem to be too little and taking too long. Would they help to rebuild communities in the style which suited the needs of the 21st Century?

The short answer is they might, but there's a way to go. For at least three reasons it is too early to say what effect the plethora of initiatives will have on the wider community:

1. The Neighbourhood Renewal Action Plan was rightly concerned not just with the amount of money spent but *how* it is spent. Local Strategic Partnerships were established involving representatives of the community and all key delivery partners across the sectors. Even the first in the field have only been effectively up and running for barely a year. The Children's Fund and the Local Network Fund have made their first grants. The funding of small community groups through this programme will build local capacity, but in years, not months. It is simply too early to make judgements about the impact of these programmes.

2. Much will depend on the attitudes of local authorities and again the jury is still out. Many of the new programmes are being driven from the centre but steered by local authorities with the clear requirement that they should include the formal voluntary sector and the wider community. Again it will take time to make judgements about the success of this process, but there is no doubt that local authorities can make it or break it.

3. Real community involvement will need real cultural change for many civil servants, locally and nationally, who have spent their entire working lives operating under a different ethos. I have heard senior ministers talk with great passion about joined-up government, community development and local involvement. Their speeches could have been written by community activists! Unfortunately, somewhere between the front bench and the frontline an enormous government machine carries on delivering just as it always has. Making money available for new programmes is relatively easy. Developing a public service culture which values initiative, encourages flexibility, and even, within reasonable bounds, embraces risk, is far more challenging and takes a lot longer.

Principles of Community Development

Progress may be slow, but our generation now has a unique opportunity to explore and develop a 21st Century definition of community and an application of that definition which is both relevant and timely. We will, however, squander that chance if we lose sight of the principles of community development. Our work is nothing if it is not based on a coherent ideology. We at Community Links identified ten principles, of which at least these four are universal.

- ## Bottom Up, Not Top Down

We all need help at some time in our lives and we all have something to give. Those who experience a problem understand it best.

These two linked ideas in the Community Links vision underpin all that we do and are reflected in our management processes. Services are not only delivered by people with first-hand experience but are also planned by them. Playschemes and After-school Clubs, for instance, are run by parents, by Leaders who were once Junior Leaders, and by Junior Leaders who were once Playscheme users. The agency Plan is not dreamt up by an exclusive team at the top but consists of many plans that are completed by people on the ground.

- ## Equal, But Different

We all have a responsibility to distinguish between the diversity that enriches our society and the inequalities that diminish it. This is about more than equal opportunities. It is also about valuing difference whilst also aggressively tackling the poverty that breeds on division.

- ## With, Not For

We don't do things *for* people. Organisations like ours might be easier to manage if we did, but they would also lose their purpose. We guide, support, train, enable, and inspire people in the belief that this is the only way to achieve lasting change. It is also hard. Many people live difficult stressful lives. Some, ground down by the process, become suspicious and cynical, others become angry – brutalised by the hostility in everything from the architecture on the tower block estates, to the attitude of the staff at the benefits agency. If you don't expect anyone to listen to you, you stop talking, but a feeling of powerlessness is not the same as apathy. We work to overcome cynicism, anger, and powerlessness, and then we encourage and enable people to take responsibility for change.

- ## Many Leaders, One Direction

Politicians and journalists like the idea of a charismatic social entrepreneur who can put the world to rights all on their own. We believe that successful community work is by definition a team effort. Community Links projects are varied because they meet a wide range of different needs. There are many leaders, but we are united by a common set of principles, and by the belief that we all have the potential to do great things – some are disadvantaged by poverty or circumstance and need advice, support, or practical help. Community Links is not primarily a building or a constitution or even a handful of leaders. It is commitment to these ideas, shared across a wide network of people and brought to life in our practical projects.

In Conclusion

As I survey the scene from London at the start of the 21st Century, I am encouraged. Certainly we have much to do. The consequences of, in the broadest sense, underinvestment in the public realm are as evident in the declining figures for voting turnout as they are in the infrastructure of the National Health Service or the public transport systems. But we have a government which has committed itself to tackling poverty and to rebuilding our poorest communities. It is easy to be cynical – politicians' promises rarely carry guarantees – but it is, I believe, better to capture and to develop limited opportunities and so to make the case for more, than to curse our ill fortune and wait for utopia.

All this that I see in the UK is occurring in the context of a global revolution. Communications, the essence of community development, have been transformed. We now have the capacity to learn from, and to share with, our fellow human beings down the street and across the planet. Thus far we have barely begun to harness the potential for the common good. It is time to revisit our definitions of community and to update our expectations of community development.

These are huge and exciting opportunities but in our enthusiasm for embracing them we must not leave behind the tried, tested, and widely-applicable principles which lie at the heart of successful and sustainable community development. Political support is opening up new opportunities for community development in the UK. Technological advances will enable us, potentially, to learn from the world, to share our learning, and to build new communities. Timeless principles will make it worthwhile.

David Robinson
Canning Town, London, 2003

Annah Mashabela

My name is Annah Mashabela. I am 43 years old and married to the priest at St John's, the blue and white Christian community, beside the tarred road. I love the word of God very much. Every day when I go to sleep, I pray, 'Thank God for protecting me in the road and giving me food to eat'

I am a teacher at Mashabela Primary School. I have five children. My mother looks after my little one, who is three; so that I can work to keep my older children in tertiary education. My husband only receives donations from the church. I am on the women's garden committee and have always been a leader with the women.

We were in the dark before. We were just sitting and doing nothing. Many people were acting to help themselves and their children, but no-one else. We now know that if you do something in your village, the things you do, must help you and help others.

We learnt a lot in the development learning group. We are now able to lead our people to accomplish things for ourselves and improve our village.

In the Church, I'm on the women's committee. Every week, we come together and contribute 20c (2p). That 20c has done a lot. We have bought 3 pots – big pots – size 30 and 2 sized 25. We have bought plates and cups and also some trunks, to keep our dishes safe. We have done all of this with our 20c. We also contribute 50c every 2 weeks so that we can help the men to build a church.

If you are united at home, everything goes smoothly. When things are not united – you just need to sit down and talk to the person – and then say 'This and that I don't like' – and then listen to what he says. In the village it is just the same. Come together and talk together so that your understanding at the end comes to a decision that everybody agrees with.

At the moment we are not united with the men. The women in the gardens do not agree with the MDC. They do not always trust the men not to eat our money. But in the end, I hope that through sitting together, they will agree.

When Sister Mary was here, she said that she would have no men – but I don't know how that will work out. Some things are difficult to do on our own. The engine in the river (irrigation pump) is very hard for us to mend. We are supposed to ask a man (to mend it) and then pay him. But if at the beginning we were allowed to mix with the men, it would be easy. Sister Mary said the men are dangerous. She told us that the men will take all our money.

It seems to me that it is a waste for the village not to be united. The women are strong enough now not to be taken over. It is difficult because I was not born here. I came here through the church and my husband.

My message to people about development:

'Work together. Talk together and sit together. You can be a prophet, a dignity man – you can be a leader. You can fly! But if you don't have love, you do it for your own sake not for another.'

Bibliography

Broadly relating to Development

Asante, M.K., *Afrocentricity* (New Jersey: Africa World Press: 1988).

Ariyaratne, A.T., *Tolerance as a Positive Characteristic for Personal and Structural Change* (New Delhi, India: UNESCO and the Department of Culture: 1995).

Ariyaratne, A.T., *Buddhist Thought in Sarvodaya Practice*, Seventh International Seminar on Buddhism and Leadership for Peace, Honolulu, Hawaii, 1995.

Berger, Peter L., *Pyramids of Sacrifice* (London: Penguin Books: 1974).

Chambers, Robert, *Rural Development. Putting the Last First* (Harlow: Longman: 1983).

Chambers, Robert, *Whose Reality Counts? Putting the First Last* (London: ITDG Publishing: 1997).

Cooke, Bill and Kothari, Uma, *Participation, The New Tyranny* (London: Zed Books: 2001).

Craig, Gary and Mayo, Marjorie (eds.) *Community Empowerment* (London: Zed Books: 1995).

Delius, Peter, *A Lion Amongst the Cattle* (Randburg: Ravan Press, South Africa: 1996).

Friere, Paulo, *Pedagogy of the Oppressed* (London: Penguin: 1972).

Hearn, Jeff, Sheppard, Deborah L., Tancred-Sheriff, Peta, and Burrell, Gibson (eds.) *The Sexuality of Organization* (London: Sage Publications: 1989).

Hope, A, Timmel, S. and Hodzi, C., *Training for Transformation: A Handbook for Community Workers* (Zimbabwe: Mambo Press: 1984).

Kaplan, Allan, *The Development Practitioners' Handbook* (London: Pluto Press: 1996).

Lean, Mary, *Bread, Bricks, and Belief: Communities in Charge of their Future* (Connecticut: Kumarian Press: 1995).

Leech, Kenneth, *Care and Conflict: Leaves from a Pastoral Notebook* (London: Darton, Longman and Todd: 1990).

Maynard, M., Purvis, J., *Researching Women's Lives from a Feminist Perspective* (London: Taylor Francis: 1994).

Putnam, Robert, *Bowling Alone: The Collapse and Revival of American Community* (New York: Simon & Schuster: 2000).

Rahman, Md. Anisur, *People's Self Development: Perspectives on Participatory Action Research (A journey through experience)* (London: Zed Books: 1993).

Rahman, Md. Anisur, 'The Case of the Third World: People's Self Development'. *Community Development Journal* Vol. 25, No. 4: p307-313.

Reason, Peter, *Human Inquiry in Action, Developments in New Paradigm Research* (London: Sage: 1988).

Sampson, Robert J. 'Transcending Tradition: New Directions in Community Research, Chicago Style'. *Criminology* 40: p213-230.

Schumacher, E.F., *Small is Beautiful, A Study of Economics as if People Mattered* (London: Abacus: 1974).

Sen, Amartya, *Development as Freedom* (Oxford: Oxford University Press: 1999).

Social Mobilisation, Reconstruction and Development, Lessons from the Mass Democratic Movement (Northern Province: SADEP and UNICEF: 1996).

Serageldin I., Barrett, R. (eds.) *Ethics and Spiritual Values: Promoting Environmentally Sustainable Development* (Washington DC: World Bank: 1995).

Whitaker, Dorothy, Stock, *Using Groups to Help People*, 2nd Edition, Brunner – (Hove, East Sussex: Routledge: 2001).

Non Development

Bateson, G. and M.C., *Mind and Nature: A Necessary Unity* (London: Wildwood House: 1979).

Chodron, P., *The Wisdom of No Escape* (Boston: Shambala: 1991).

Frankl, Victor E., *Man's Search for Meaning* (New York: Touchstone: 1959).

Goldberg, N., *Writing Down The Bones* (Boston: Shambala: 1986).

Hookham, M., *On Freeing the Heart* (Oxford: Longchen Foundation: 1985).

Kabat-Zinn, J., *Wherever You Go, There You Are* (New York: Hyperion: 1994).

Kornfield. J., *A Path with Heart: A Guide through the Perils and Promises of Spiritual Life* (New York: Bantam: 1994).

Lewis, T., Amini, F., Lannon, R., *A General Theory of Love* (New York: Vintage Books: 2000).

Nisargadatta, Maharaj, *I Am That* (Durham, US: The Acorn Press: 1973).

Oliver, M., *New and Selected Poems* (Boston: Beacon: 1992).

Rilke, Rainer Maria, *Book of Hours: Love Poems to God* translated by Anita Barrows and Joanna Macy (New York: Riverhead Books: 1996).

Rumi, *The Essential Rumi* translated by Coleman Barks with John Moyne (London: Penguin: 1995).

Shikpo, Rigdzin, *Openness, Clarity and Sensitivity* (Oxford: Longchen Foundation: 1992).

Suzuki, S., *Zen Mind, Beginner's Mind* (New York: Weatherhill Inc: 1970).

Related Websites

Community Links (Publishers/Community Development, UK),
www.community-links.org

OLIVE, Organisation Development and Training (South Africa), www.oliveodt.co.za

Trish Bartley (Author), www.trishbartley.co.uk

Books for Africa, www.booksforafrica.org

Book Aid, www.bookaid.org

Training, Research and Resources in Awareness/Mindfulness

North Wales Centre for Mindfulness, www.bangor.ac.uk/mindfulness

Centre for Mindfulness, Massachusetts, www.umassmed.edu.cfm

Notes

Preface

1. Lean, Mary, *Bread, Bricks and Belief. Communities in Charge of their Future* (Connecticut: Kumarian Press Inc.: 1995, p37).

Introduction

1. Rilke, Rainer Maria, *Book of Hours: Love Poems to God* translated by Anita Barrows and Joanna Macy (New York: Riverhead Books: 1996, p63).

2. Rahman, Md. Anisur, *People's Self Development: Perspectives on Participatory Action Research (A journey through experience)* (London: Zed Books: 1993).

3. Sampson, Robert J., 2002. 'Transcending Tradition: New Directions in Community Research, Chicago Style'. *Criminology*, 40: p213-230.

4. Bateson, Gregory and Mary, *Mind and Nature: Necessary Unity* (London: Wildwood House: 1979).

Chapter 1 – The Community and the Development Practitioner

1. Delius, Peter, *A Lion amongst the Cattle, Reconstruction and Resistance in the Northern Transvaal* (Johannesburg: Ravan Press 1996).

2. ibid

3. Rahman, Md. Anisur, 'The Case of the Third World: People's Self Development. *Community Development Journal* Vol. 25, No. 4, (1990) p307-313.

Chapter 2 – The Development Story

1. Castaneda, Carlos, *The Teachings of Don Juan* (London: Arkana, Penguin: 1968).

2. African proverb.

Chapter 3 – The Learning

1. Eliot, T.S., Extract from East Coker from The Four Quartets. *Collected Poems 1909-1962.* (Faber and Faber)

2. Rahman Md. Anisur, *People's Self Development: Perspective on Participatory Action Research. (A journey through experience)* (London: Zed Books: 1993)

3. Kaplan, Allan, *The Development Practitioner's Handbook* (London: Pluto Press: 1996)

4. I am grateful to Ken and Elizabeth Mellor (www.biamenetwork.net) who first introduced me to this model. I have adapted it slightly.

5. Morgan, Gareth, *Beyond Meaning.* (London: Sage: 1983)

6. I would like to thank Loretta van Schalkwyk for her support in developing this model.

7. Kolb, D.A. *Experiential Learning. Experience as the source of learning and development* (New Jersey: Prentice Hall: 1984)

8. Lieberman, M.A. Lakin, M. and Whitaker,D.S. The Group as a Unique Context for Therapy', *Psychotherapy: Theory Research and Practice* (1968: p29-36)

9. Rahman, Md. Anisur, *People's Self Development: Perspective on Participatory Action Research. (A journey through experience)* (London: Zed Books: 1993)

10. Chambers, Robert, *Rural Development – Putting the Last First* (London: Longman, Scientific and Technical: 1983)

11. Rogers, Carl, The Characteristics of a Helping Relationship, *Personnel and Guidance Journal*, Vol 37: 1958, p6-16. (American Association for Counselling and Development)

12. Lewis, Thomas, Amini, Fari, Lannon, Richard, *A General Theory of Love* (New York, Vintage Books: 2001)

13. Lukes, Steven S., *Power: A Radical View.* (London: MacMIlllan Press, Ltd.: 1974).

14. Arendt, Hannah, *The Human Condition* (Chicago and London: University of Chicago Press: 1958)

15. Tutu, Desmond Mpilo, 'Viability' in Relevant Theology for Africa: Report on a Consultation of the Missiological Institutue at Lutheran Theological College, Mapumulo, Natal 12-21 September 1972, Hans-Jurgemn Becken (ed.), (Durban, Lutheran Publishing House: 1973, p38).

16. Hulley, Leonard, Kretzschmar, Louise, Pato, Luke Lungile (Eds.) *Archbishop Tutu: Prophetic Witness in South Africa.* (Cape Town, Human and Rousseau: 1996, p16)

17. Mbiti, John, *African religions and philosophies* (New York: Doubleday and Company: 1970, p141).

18. Heaney, Tom, Freirean, Tom, *Literacy in North America: The Community-Based Education Movement Thresholds in Education* (1989) http://nlu.nl.edu/ace/Resources/Documents/FreireIssues/html

19. Sen, Amartya, *Development as Freedom* (Oxford, NY: Oxford University Press: 1999, p295).

20. Putnam, R.D. *Bowling Alone. The Collapse and Revival of American community* (New York: Simon and Schuster: 2000).

21. Buber, Martin. *Tales of the Hasidim: Early Masters* (New York: Schocken: 1947). Transl. O. Marx. 1947).

22. From the *Book of Common Prayer*.

23. Heron, John, *The Facilitator's Handbook* (London: Kogan Page: 1986).

24. Paulo Freire Institute, Purpose and Objectives www.paulofreire.org/objectives.htm

25. Smith, M.K. 'Martin Buber on education', The encyclopedia of informal education, http://www.infed.org/ thinkers/et-buber.htm (2000).

26. Rumi, translated by Coleman Barks, *The Essential Rumi* (London: Penguin: 1995).

Chapter 4 – The Principles

1. Rilke, Rainer Maria, *Book of Hours: Love Poems to God* Translated by Anita Barrows and Joanna Macy (New York: Riverhead Books: 1996, p58).

2. *World Development Report, 1997* (Washington DC, USA: World Bank).

3. Arnstein, Sherry R. 'A Ladder of Citizen Participation,' *Journal of the American Planning Association*, Vol. 35, No. 4, July 1969: pp216-224.

4. Rumi, translated by Coleman Barks, *The Essential Rumi* (London: Penguin: 1995).

5. Williamson Marianne, *A Return to Love; Reflections on the Principles of A Course in Miracles* (New York: Harper Collins: 1992) (often attributed to Nelson Mandela's presidential inauguration speech in 1994).

6. Oliver, Mary, Wild Geese from *New and Selected Poems* (Boston: Beacon Press: 1992: p110.

7. Chopra, Deepak, *Ageless Body Timeless Mind* (London: Rider: 1993, p319).

8. Schumacher, E.F., *Small is Beautiful: A Study of Economics as if People Mattered* (London: Abacus: 1974, p27).

Chapter 5 – Conclusion

1. Rilke, Rainer Maria, *Book of Hours: Love Poems to God*, Translated by Anita Barrows and Joanna Macy (New York: Riverhead Books: 1996, p51).

2. Rumi, *The Essential Rumi*, Translated by Coleman Barks with John Moyne (London: Penguin: 1996).

Chapter 6 – The Contexts

1. Putnam, Robert, *Bowling Alone: The Collapse and Revival of American Community* (New York: Simon & Schuster: 2000).

Index